From Birth To First Words

Activities to Support Your Baby's Language Learning

In the First Year of Life

Lynn Carson, M.Cl.Sc., S-LP (C)

FROM BIRTH TO FIRST WORDS. Copyright © 2019

All rights reserved. No part of this book may be used or reproduced in any manner whatsoever without written permission except in the case of brief quotations embodied in critical articles and reviews.

Every effort has been made to ensure that the content provided in this book is accurate and helpful to readers, however this book is not intended as a substitute for medical advice. The reader should consult a physician or specialist in matters relating to the health or development of their child, particularly with respect to any symptoms that may require a diagnosis or medical attention. Neither the author nor the publisher claims responsibility for adverse effects resulting from the use of the information found with this book or that of the resources provided.

ISBN: 9781797670195

This book is dedicated to my children, who allowed me the pleasure of accompanying them on their language learning journeys, and to my husband, whose limitless love and support gave me the chance to do so.

CONTENTS

A LETTER TO PARENTS FROM THE AUTHOR 1

HELPFUL INFORMATION TO KNOW BEFORE USING THIS BOOK 3

1 LISTENING TO SOUNDS – BECOMING PART OF THE WORLD OF TALKING 6

NEWBORN 7
Week 1: Let's Get To Know Each Other 8
Week 2: Bath Time Talk 9
Week 3: My First Story Time Routine 10
Week 4: Lullaby And Goodnight 11

1 MONTH OLD 15
Week 5: Pick Your Moment – Reading Baby's Cues 16
Week 6: Talk "Baby Talk" To Me 17
Week 7: Little Copycat 18
Week 8: Mealtime Talk – It's All In The Eyes 19

2 MONTHS OLD 23
Week 9: Dress Me Up Rhyme Time 24
Week 10: Cozy Chats – Listen For The Coo 25
Week 11: Sounds All Around – A Listening Game 26
Week 12: Little Lip Reader 27

3 MONTHS OLD 31
Week 13: Singing For Sounds – A Vowel Encouragement Game 32
Week 14: Bringing Out The Social Smile 33
Week 15: Mirror Peek-A-Boo 34
Week 16: Funny Finger Plays – Watch With Me 35

3 MONTH MILESTONES AND MEMORIES 36

2 IT'S ABOUT TO GET NOISY – LEARNING TO USE THEIR VOICE 38

4 MONTHS OLD 39
Week 17: Tickle Turns – Listen For The Laugh 40
Week 18: Let's Get Noisy Baby! – Exploring Sounds In Vocal Play 41
Week 19: Everyday Storyteller – Narrating Daily Routines 42
Week 20: Our First Game – Baby Bubble Play 43

5 MONTHS OLD — 47
Week 21: Mommy/Daddy The Mime – Adding Gestures To Everyday Talk — 48
Week 22: Own Name Hide And Seek — 49
Week 23: You Reach, Then I Teach – In Play — 50
Week 24: Let's Play Ball – A Turn Taking Game — 51

6 MONTHS OLD — 55
Week 25: Copy Me – The Musical Kitchen — 56
Week 26: The Bath Time Babble Box — 57
Week 27: You Reach, Then I Teach – With Books — 58
Week 28: What I Have Learned So Far – Quiz — 59

6 MONTH MILESTONES AND MEMORIES — 63

3 LEARNING THE MEANING OF WORDS — 66

7 MONTHS OLD — 67
Week 29: Tidy Up Time – Increasing The Daily Dose Of Songs — 68
Week 30: The Discovery Drawer – Using Parallel Talk — 69
Week 31: You're The Boss – Reverse Imitation — 70
Week 32: Baby Art – A Vessel For Vocabulary — 71

8 MONTHS OLD — 77
Week 33: Monkey See Monkey Do – An Imitation Game — 78
Week 34: What Will We Read Today? – Baby's Choice — 79
Week 35: "Going To Get Your…" - A Verbal Routine — 80
Week 36: Making Informed Choices In A Digital Age – Screen Time Quiz — 81

9 MONTHS OLD — 85
Week 37: Puppet Jargon — 86
Week 38: The Family Fort — 87
Week 39: Peter Pointer Bedtime Routine — 88
Week 40: Books O' Plenty — 89

9 MONTH MILESTONES AND MEMORIES — 93

4 GETTING READY TO SAY FIRST WORDS — 96

10 MONTHS OLD — 97
Week 41: My Little Helper — 98
Week 42: Follow The Leader – Understanding Baby's Nonverbal Communication — 99
Week 43: Tower, Talk And Tumble — 100
Week 44: Choice Of Two, What Will You Do? — 101

11 MONTHS OLD ... 107
Week 45: Rule Of Thumb Is 5:1 ... 108
Week 46: Silly Sounds With Play Dough ... 109
Week 47: A Little Bit Of Sabotage Goes A Long Way ... 110
Week 48: Peek-A-Boo "Hi" And "Bye" ... 111

12 MONTHS OLD ... 115
Week 49: Fill It In Baby ... 116
Week 50: Our Daily Talking Game ... 117
Week 51: Word Toss – Teaching Early Categories ... 118
Week 52: Let's Pretend – Ready, Set, Copy Me ... 119

12 MONTH MILESTONES AND MEMORIES ... 123

WORD TRACKER ... 126
FINAL THOUGHTS ... 127

APPENDIX ... 129
Trouble Shooting Strategies ... 130
Resources – Recommended Books And Websites ... 131
Regulatory Bodies For Speech-Language Pathologists And Audiologists ... 132
What To Expect In The Next Year – 12-24 Month Milestones ... 133
What To Do If You Have Concerns About Your Child's Language Development ... 134
Key Terms ... 135

References ... 137
Picture References ... 146
Acknowledgements ... 148
About The Author ... 149

A LETTER TO PARENTS FROM THE AUTHOR

Let me begin by saying congratulations on the arrival of a beautiful new addition to your family! You and your baby are about to embark on a wonderful journey together over the next year; learning about one another, sharing experiences together and discovering a new world as parent and child.

There is so much learning that will take place over this next year it can be hard to imagine. Your baby will learn to eat, drink from a cup, roll over, grasp objects, crawl, walk, and play. With all this change going on (accompanied by many sleepless nights for both baby and parent) it can be hard to remember that the first year is also an important one in your baby's language development. In fact, it might be hard to believe, but your adorable little bundle will be doing some of the most rapid language learning during the next five years than at any other point in their life. Amazing!

When you look down at this tiny person starting out in the world, it can be easy to believe that they are just passive observers, and language development isn't something a parent needs to consider in these early months. In fact nothing could be further from the truth. Your baby's brain will work actively every day to learn to talk, and they'll rely on you to help them. That's why along with loving and caring for your baby, you are also their first and most important teacher. The types of experiences you provide them with, how often you talk to them, and the quality of talk you provide, all shape how fast and how well your baby will develop language skills during their first year and beyond.

Ludwig Wittgenstein, the Austrian-British philosopher once said, "The limits of my language mean the limits of my world." I have come to believe wholeheartedly that this is true, both through my experience as a speech-language pathologist and as a mother. Language is the way we connect as human beings. It is the tool with which we both interpret, and engage with the world around us. So, to me, it makes sense that the better you are at using this tool, the more successful you're likely to be at negotiating whatever life has in store for you. In fact, increasingly more and more research is providing evidence that supports this idea. Studies show that children with strong early language skills are more likely to have better reading skills at school age, gain higher academic achievement, possess stronger social skills and earn better wages as adults. And it all begins by helping them reach that special milestone of saying their first word.

Before you use this book it is important to understand three truths:

>Truth #1: Babies start learning language from the moment they are born.

>Truth #2: It is expected that babies say their first word between 9-14 months old.

>Truth #3: There is a HUGE amount of language learning that must occur before a baby can

say their first word and it is largely learned through the experiences they have with the adults in their lives.

A final thing to keep in mind is that this book was designed to be a helpful tool for you to use over the course of your baby's first year. It was *not* written to help you become an expert in speech and language development. It was also *not* meant to overwhelm you with yet another task to do each day. As a parent of two, I know you don't need to add more complications into this busy time. The purpose of this book is to suggest simple ways you can help your baby learn to talk in a way that works well for both you and your growing infant.

Inside you will find reliable information about typical early language development, so you can feel more knowledgeable as you support your baby through each stage. There are also areas that allow you to not only track your baby's speech and language milestones as they occur, but to capture these memories as keepsakes that will last a lifetime. Finally, and most importantly, there are simple yet powerful research-based activities to support your baby's language development for each week of their first year. All activities can be easily incorporated into daily living routines and are designed specifically to age and stage of development. There are also extension activities offered if you feel you are ready to do a little more.

It is my hope that this book empowers you as a parent, to feel confident in your ability to support your child's language development from the moment they are born. And when you do watch your child reach that remarkable milestone of saying their first word, you will know you helped them to build a strong foundation in language so they can move forward in their next year of life as a confident communicator!

Wishing you, your baby and your family, a lifetime of love and learning together beginning with this very special first year.

    Lynn Carson, M.Cl.Sc., S-LP(C)

HELPFUL INFORMATION TO KNOW BEFORE USING THIS BOOK

What will I find in this book?

- A simple, research-based, language learning activity to do with your baby for each week of their first year that can all be easily incorporated into daily living routines.
- Speech and language milestone tracking charts at 3, 6, 9, 12 and 24 months so you can make sure your baby's speech and language development stays on track.
- Resource lists for books, websites, toy recommendations and more to enrich what you are doing with your baby each week.
- Recommendations on what to do if your baby does not meet a milestone or is not talking.
- And much, much more!

When should I do these activities?

These activities have been designed to be easily incorporated into typical daily routines. Each week you will be introduced to a new activity to build into your day, so that by the end of the year you will be doing 52 easy, yet powerful language boosting activities with your baby each day.

How long will these activities take?

Each activity takes between 1-5 minutes to do, however you can continue the activity even longer if your baby is enjoying themselves and wants to engage more, or you can repeat the activity more than once in a day. There are also extension activities offered so you can continue the same language boosting technique in slightly different ways.

Do I need to buy special toys or other items to do the activities in this book?

Absolutely not! For most of the activities in this book all you need are you and your baby. Other activities may require typical items you can find around the house. Toy ideas are suggested but they are not a requirement to accomplish the activities in this book.

How am I supposed to use this book in my daily life with my new baby?

Place this book somewhere you can easily access it. Each week read the recommended activity then practice this activity every day with your baby. Sometimes I will recommend a specific time in the day to do an activity, however feel free to choose when and how to build these activities into your day so it works well for you and your family. Add new language boosting activities into your routine each week as your baby grows while continuing with the ones learned from the previous weeks.

As you progress through the book, track your baby's speech and language milestones and celebrate these special moments by adding a picture of your baby at that age and writing down any special memories. Shortly after you have completed the book (or maybe even before) you will have heard your baby's first words. Not only will you have a beautiful memory book of their journey towards this special time in their lives to keep forever, but you will be prepared as their parent and teacher to help them become confident communicators as they learn to say so much more.

What should I do if I'm having trouble with any of the activities?

Even with the best intentions, when it comes to babies, things sometimes don't always go as planned. If you are having trouble with any of the recommended activities try reviewing the Trouble Shooting Strategies (p.130) in the appendix of this book.

Sounds great! Do you have any tips before I begin?

- **Be flexible!** All babies are unique and will respond differently to the activities. Read your baby's cues and use your understanding of their special personality to help you tailor the recommended activities to fit them.
- **Be committed!** You really don't have to be a speech-language pathologist to help your baby develop strong early language skills, but it does require two important things. First, a little bit of reliable knowledge about how to support early speech and language development, which you will find in this book, and second, the dedication and love to teach your baby each day. A few minutes a day is such a small amount of time to give, but it can make a lifetime's worth of difference to a child's language development.
- **Have fun!** These activities can only take you so far. The most important thing is that you are enjoying being a part of this language-learning journey with your baby. If you are having fun and are engaged, chances are, your baby will be too!

LISTENING TO SOUNDS

BECOMING PART OF THE WORLD OF TALKING

NEWBORN

WEEK 1: LET'S GET TO KNOW EACH OTHER

AREA ADDRESSED – Expressive Language

SKILL TARGETED - Cries for specific needs

WHY DO THIS? - One of the first things you will notice when you bring your new baby home is that they cry. Babies will cry for a variety of different reasons such as hunger, pain or fatigue. Although all babies cry to have their needs met, because each baby is unique, how often and when they cry will be different. By watching and listening to your baby, and then responding appropriately to meet their needs, you're not only caring for them, but are also beginning to teach them that their vocal behaviour can have an effect on a listener. Research has shown that parents who are consistently responsive and accurate in identifying their infant's needs during the first year, had babies who cried less at 12 months and were also more communicative.

THINGS YOU NEED - Yourself, baby, pen, Getting To Know Each Other worksheet (p.12)

SPECIAL THINGS TO REMEMBER - Understanding why a newborn baby is crying takes time and practice. Read your baby's other behaviour cues (e.g., facial expressions, body movements) and the environment (e.g. too noisy, too cold or too hot, too bright, etc.) to help give you clues as to what your baby needs.

ACTIVITY – As you care for your baby this week, use the Getting To Know Each Other worksheet to help you figure out why your baby might be crying and how you could respond to their needs. Record any unique things your baby does to let you know they need something.

MY BABY WILL - Cry throughout the day in response to behaviour needs, for example hunger, fatigue, over stimulation, under stimulation, discomfort or seeking closeness.

THEN I WILL - Respond immediately to my baby's cry and address their needs. For example, feeding them if I think they are crying because of hunger or cuddling them if I think they are crying to seek closeness.

TIP

Sometimes newborn babies cry and it can be very challenging to figure out what they need. If you ever have questions or concerns about how often your baby cries, talk to your doctor.

WEEK 2: BATH TIME TALK

AREA ADDRESSED – Phonological Development

SKILL TARGETED - Hearing the sounds of language

WHY DO THIS? – Before babies say their first words they need to learn all the different speech sounds in their language(s). They start learning speech sounds from the moment they are born by listening to you speak. Although it may seem surprising, while you talk to your baby their brain is working hard to actively process all the speech sounds they hear you say, so they can one day use these sounds themselves to talk to you.

THINGS YOU NEED - Yourself, baby, tub and soft cloth

SPECIAL THINGS TO REMEMBER - Setting up a routine for dedicated face-to-face talking is a great first step to ensure lots of talking exposure in these early months. Bath time is a wonderful regular routine to build talking time into since babies are typically alert during this time. If your baby does not like the bath and fusses or cries when in the water, perhaps have special talking time just before or just after the bath. It does not matter what you talk about since babies do not understand word meanings yet, so go ahead and speak freely and enjoy this special early talking time with your new baby.

ACTIVITY – Get the bath ready for your baby with required bath items all prepared beforehand so you are not searching for things as you bathe and can focus on talking. Gently place your baby in the tub. Begin the bath time routine and talking with your baby.

MY BABY WILL – Go into the bath and perhaps wiggle and move. They will look up at my face and around the room as I bathe them.

THEN I WILL – Begin to talk to my baby about whatever comes naturally. I will use facial expressions and variations in my voice to keep my baby interested as I talk and bathe them.

TIP

Make sure you and baby are in comfortable positions and that you are face-to-face.

WEEK 3: MY FIRST STORY TIME ROUTINE

AREA ADDRESSED – Early Literacy

SKILL TARGETED – Experience with reading materials

WHY DO THIS? – Studies show that the earlier children are exposed to book reading and the more they are read to, the better their language and literacy skills are later on. In fact, parents who started reading to their children as infants had babies who went on to talk more and have larger vocabularies as toddlers and preschoolers.

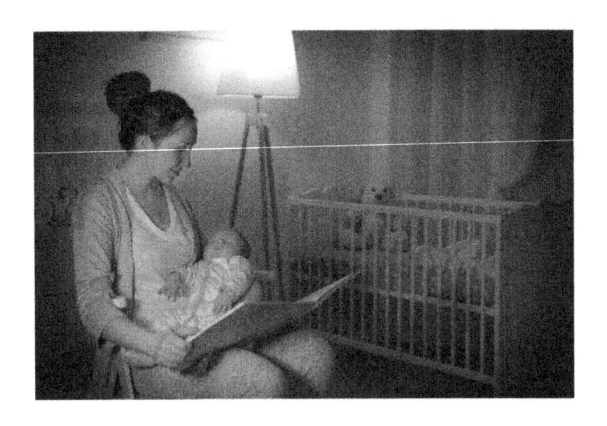

THINGS YOU NEED – Yourself, baby and reading material

SPECIAL THINGS TO REMEMBER – At this stage your baby is not awake for very long and can't see pictures on the page very clearly, so feel free to choose reading material that suits your own personal interests. The important thing is to develop a reading routine that works for you and your new baby that you can continue through their first year and beyond.

ACTIVITY – Choose something to read. It can be a book for babies or something you would like to read (e.g., magazines, newspaper, etc.). Choose a time in your daily routine that works well to offer dedicated daily reading time with your baby (e.g., when baby first wakes up or just before bedtime). Find a quiet place to sit or lay down with your baby. Bring them in close to you and begin to read aloud.

MY BABY WILL – Be awake and calm before we begin reading together. They may want to be cuddled, be wrapped up or want to stretch out. Allow your baby to get in a comfortable position before reading.

THEN I WILL – Get in a comfortable position with my baby and begin reading softly and slowly in a soothing voice.

TIP

Reading to a baby at this stage will be short and may only last a couple of minutes. Continue reading aloud for as long as your baby is content to listen. Look for fussing or crying to occur as your baby signals they are ready for story time to be over.

WEEK 4: LULLABY AND GOODNIGHT

AREA ADDRESSED - Receptive Language

SKILL TARGETED - Quiets to a familiar voice

WHY DO THIS? – Infants do not yet understand the meaning of words. Tone of voice is one of the first ways they begin to connect emotion and meaning to the speech sounds they hear. Newborn babies can already recognize the loving and soothing tone in lullabies sung to them by adults, and with repetition learn to calm down in response to this caring message being expressed to them.

THINGS YOU NEED - Yourself and baby

SPECIAL THINGS TO REMEMBER - Babies don't care if their parents can carry a tune. They respond to the calm, soothing nature of the tone of voice. When singing, keep your voice soft and melodic to send the message to your baby that they are safe and you will help comfort them.

ACTIVITY - When your baby is showing signs of being tired (e.g., crying, fussing), pick them up and hold them close. Begin to sing softly to them. Some babies also like to be walked around or rocked to help them feel comforted. Even if your baby continues to cry for a little while when you begin the song, keep singing softly and calmly until they settle down.

MY BABY WILL – Cry or fuss indicating they are tired and ready to sleep.

THEN I WILL – Begin singing and cuddling my baby to help them begin to settle down, become quiet and perhaps fall asleep.

TIP

Different babies will respond to different song tempos. This week use the lullaby example list (p.13) to explore which song your baby prefers.

GETTING TO KNOW EACH OTHER

My baby might cry because of:
- hunger
- fatigue
- the environment being uncomfortable (ex: hot, cold, noisy, bright lights)
- their body being uncomfortable (ex: gas, bowel movement, dirty diaper, itchy, sick, pain)
- to seek closeness or attention

Things I might see my baby do:
- rub their eyes or yawn if they are tired
- suck their fingers or fist or turn their head towards my chest if they are hungry
- squirm or turn their head if they are uncomfortable
- cough or sneeze if they are sick
- arch their back or pull their legs up if they are in pain

Responses I could try might be:
- hold my baby close or rock my baby and sing softly
- feed my baby
- make changes to the environment
- change my baby's diaper
- check my baby's temperature
- check my baby's body
- talk to my baby
- gently burp my baby

Other things I learned about my baby this week:
_____
_____
_____
_____
_____
_____

LULLABIES

HUSH LITTLE BABY	**TWINKLE TWINKLE**
Hush, little baby, don't say a word, Papa's gonna buy you a mockingbird. And if that mockingbird won't sing, Papa's gonna buy you a diamond ring. And if that diamond ring turns brass, Papa's gonna buy you a looking glass. And if that looking glass gets broke, Papa's gonna buy you a billy goat. And if that billy goat won't pull, Papa's gonna buy you a cart and bull. And if that cart and bull turn over, Papa's gonna buy you a dog named Rover. And if that dog named Rover won't bark, Papa's gonna buy you a horse and cart. And if that horse and cart fall down, You'll still be the sweetest baby in town.	Twinkle twinkle, little star, How I wonder what you are. Up above the world so high, Like a diamond in the sky. Twinkle twinkle, little star, How I wonder what you are.
YOU ARE MY SUNSHINE	**BAA BAA BLACK SHEEP**
You are my sunshine My only sunshine. You make me happy When skies are grey. You'll never know, dear, How much I love you. Please don't take My sunshine away.	Baa, baa, black sheep, have you any wool? Yes sir, yes sir, three bags full! One for the master, One for the dame, And one for the little boy Who lives down the lane. Baa, baa, black sheep, have you any wool? Yes sir, yes sir, Three bags full.

1 MONTH OLD

WEEK 5: PICK YOUR MOMENT – READING BABY'S CUES

AREA ADDRESSED – Phonological Development

SKILL TARGETED – Hearing the sounds of language

WHY DO THIS? – Talking with your baby is absolutely the best way to help them learn all the speech sounds they need to know in order to talk. However, did you know there are certain times to talk with your baby that are better than others? Choosing when to talk to your baby depends on their state of arousal. Understanding what state of arousal your baby is in, will help you respond accurately to their needs and help you know when your baby is most ready to listen and play with you. When they are ready to listen, these are the best language boosting moments, so talk freely and often during these times in the day.

THINGS YOU NEED – Yourself and baby

SPECIAL THINGS TO REMEMBER – Research suggests that babies will cycle through these states of arousal multiple times throughout the day. Some babies cycle through each state of arousal more quickly, while others may stay in certain states longer. How long and how often a baby will stay in each state will also change as they grow and go through different stages of development.

ACTIVITY – Use the Infant States Of Arousal chart (p.20) as a guide through the week to see how often your baby cycles through each state of arousal in a day. Pay particular attention to identifying when your baby is in the quiet alert state since this is the best time for talking and playing with them. When they are, take a few minutes to come face-to-face and speak to them about whatever you want.

MY BABY WILL – Cycle through different states of arousal throughout the day.

THEN I WILL – Respond appropriately to my baby's needs while they are in that state of arousal (e.g., put them to sleep when they are tired or interact with them when they are ready to listen). When they are in the quiet alert state I will use this opportunity for lots of talking time.

TIP

Talk with other family members about how your baby moves through each state of arousal, and why the quiet alert phase is the best language learning moment.

WEEK 6: TALK "BABY TALK" TO ME

AREA ADDRESSED – Phonological Development

SKILL TARGETED – Hearing the sounds of language

WHY DO THIS? – Young babies are more interested in listening to infant-directed speech (a.k.a. motherese or baby talk) than other types of talking. When adults use this form of talk, sounds and words stand out more clearly compared to talking to them using the same speech style you would with an adult. Babies use the cues they hear in infant-directed speech to help them learn speech sounds as young infants and learn words when they are a little older.

> **"Baby Talk" Sounds Like…**
>
> Higher pitch
> Exaggerated pronunciation
> Shorter phrases
> Repetition of words or phrases
> Longer pauses
> Sing-song voice quality

THINGS YOU NEED – Yourself and baby

SPECIAL THINGS TO REMEMBER – For some adults using infant-directed speech comes more naturally and for others it doesn't. If you are uncomfortable using infant-directed speech you don't need to do it all the time. Save this form of talk for special private moments between you and your baby.

ACTIVITY – When your baby wakes up from a nap, this is a great time to interact with them since they are unlikely to be hungry and are well rested. Place your baby on their back, either on the floor or in your lap, and get face-to-face. Talk to your baby about anything you want using infant-directed speech. You could talk about what is happening in the environment around them, what happened in your day, or how much you love them.

MY BABY WILL – Gaze into my eyes and watch my facial expressions. They may also make noises, such as burps, coughs or hiccups.

THEN I WILL – Use infant-directed speech to talk to my baby until they show signs they have had enough talking time, for example by crying or fussing.

TIP

Try and incorporate infant-directed speech into other daily routines but remember to keep all your sentences grammatically correct.

WEEK 7: LITTLE COPYCAT

AREA ADDRESSED – Pragmatic/Social Language

SKILL TARGETED – Imitates facial expressions

WHY DO THIS? – Imitation is the basis for learning. Human beings observe other people and imitate what they do or say in order to learn new skills, and this includes learning how to talk. Encouraging infants to copy behaviours helps develop their imitation skills and is also the beginning of engaging them in back-and-forth social interactions. Research has shown that even a newborn baby can imitate adult behaviours, such as sticking out their tongue.

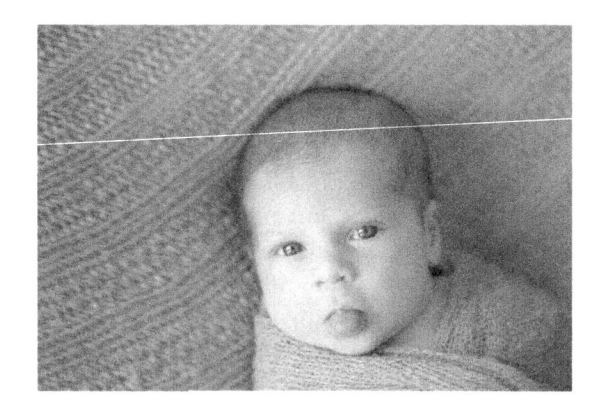

THINGS YOU NEED – Yourself and baby

SPECIAL THINGS TO REMEMBER – It may take several repeated attempts before your baby imitates you. Repeat the action slowly with a 3-5 second pause between repetitions. This gives your infant lots of time to coordinate their own body movements to imitate you back.

ACTIVITY – During diaper changing come face-to-face with your baby and tell them you are going to play a copycat game together. Then, stick out your tongue and hold it out for 2 or 3 seconds before pulling it back into your mouth. Repeat this action until your baby imitates you in return or loses interest in the activity (e.g., by crying or fussing).

MY BABY WILL – Watch my mouth and face closely then attempt to stick their tongue out too.

THEN I WILL – Smile and praise my baby for being such a good little copycat! I will repeat the activity for as long as my baby continues to enjoy the interaction.

TIP

Try to see if your baby can copy other family members too!

WEEK 8: MEALTIME TALK – IT'S ALL IN THE EYES

AREA ADDRESSED – Pragmatic/Social Language

SKILL TARGETED – Makes eye contact with an adult

WHY DO THIS? – At birth babies are able to focus a distance of 20-30cm, which is approximately the same distance between a baby's face and their parent's when in a feeding position. Talking to your baby and making eye contact with them during these moments encourages them to look at your face and make eye contact with you in return. Making eye contact is one of the most basic, but important skills we do as humans during effective communication.

THINGS YOU NEED – Yourself, baby, other feeding materials if required

SPECIAL THINGS TO REMEMBER – It doesn't really matter what you talk about since your baby does not understand the meaning of words yet. Just talk about whatever comes naturally to you in the moment. The goal is to use your tone of voice and facial expressions to encourage your baby to look into your eyes.

ACTIVITY – When your baby is hungry pick them up and begin to feed them. Get in a comfortable position for both you and your baby and then begin to talk to them in a soothing voice or using infant-directed speech.

MY BABY WILL – Gaze up into my eyes while feeding.

THEN I WILL – Use my voice and facial expressions to encourage my baby to continue making eye contact with me. I will discontinue the activity when my baby falls asleep or signals they are ready for quiet (e.g., fussing or turning away).

TIP

Save this activity for during the day when you and your baby are both more alert.

INFANT STATES OF AROUSAL

Deep Sleep	Light Sleep	Drowsy
Lies quietly with no movement, eyes are closed, breathing is deep and regular, baby may have brief startles but does not wake up.	Baby moves while sleeping, eyes are closed, may startle at noises or have bodily twitches, facial movements include frowns, grimaces, smiles, twitches, mouth movements and sucking.	Eyes may open and close but may not focus on anything in particular, body may move smoothly and quietly, breathing is irregular, may be roused to alertness or drift to sleep.
Quiet Alert	**Active Alert**	**Crying**
Body and face are relatively quiet and inactive, eyes may be trying to focus, sights and sounds will produce predictable responses. This is the state in which your baby is most amenable to play and interaction with an adult.	This is a state before crying, may be soothed or brought to a quiet alert state by attractive stimuli. However, if stimuli are too overwhelming baby may break down to fussiness.	Baby will cry, perhaps scream. Different types of cries communicate hunger, pain, boredom, discomfort and tiredness.

It is important to remember that each baby is unique, so how often and how long a baby remains or changes between these states, will depend on their personality and stage of development.

Learning your baby's signals for when they are in each state will help you know how to provide an appropriate response to meet their needs and let them know you understand their messages, helping to set the foundation for communication and language development.

Adapted from Paul, R. (2007). Language Disorders From Infancy Through Adolescence.

SPEECH SOUNDS IN ENGLISH

Speech sounds are called phonemes. There are approximately 44 speech sounds (or phonemes) in the English language represented by 26 letters of the alphabet. Infants learn speech sounds on their journey to first words by listening to adults talk to them during the back-and-forth interactions they have each day.

Speech Sound Example	Speech Sound Example
Vowels	Consonants
*C*a*t*	*B*all
P*e*t	*D*og
T*i*p	*F*it
H*o*t	*G*oat
F*u*n	*H*appy
B*oo*k	*J*ump
*Aw*ful	*K*ick
	*L*amp
T*a*ke	*M*ouse
B*ee*	*N*o
K*i*te	Thi*ng*
B*o*ne	*P*our
T*u*ne	*R*oll
C*oi*n	*S*un
C*ow*	*T*ail
	*V*anish
R controlled vowels	*W*et
C*ar*	*Y*ou
B*ir*d	*Z*oo
C*ur*e	Trea*s*ure
F*ear*	
Fl*oor*	Diagraphs
C*are*	
	*Ch*eese
	*Sh*oe
	Ba*th*
	*Th*is

21

2 MONTHS OLD

WEEK 9: DRESS ME UP RHYME TIME

AREA ADDRESSED – Phonological Development

SKILL TARGETED – Becomes familiar with speech sound combinations in language

WHY DO THIS? – In order for your baby to say their first word, they need to learn all the speech sounds in their native language(s) and how these sounds can be put together to form words. Each language has special rules for how speech sounds can be put together and these rules are called phonotactics. For example, there are no words in the English language that begin with the speech sounds zl and kp, but there are in Polish or West African languages. When an adult recites a nursery rhyme to an infant, their brain starts to use clues, like repetition and the melody of the rhyme, to begin to figure out which speech sound combinations go together to form words for their own language(s).

> **These Are Baby's Fingers**
>
> These are baby's fingers (touch baby's fingers),
> These are baby's toes (touch baby's toes),
> This is baby's belly button (touch belly button),
> Round and round it goes!
>
> These are baby's eyes (touch above eyes),
> This is baby's nose (touch nose),
> This is baby's belly button (touch belly button),
> Round and round it goes!

THINGS YOU NEED - Yourself, baby, clothes

SPECIAL THINGS TO REMEMBER – Daily nursery rhymes are important for healthy language development from birth all the way through to the preschool years. Engaging children in nursery rhymes each day teaches them the sounds of language early on, and also helps support their vocabulary, narrative language and early literacy development as they get older.

ACTIVITY – Get face-to-face when dressing your baby and make eye contact with them. During your dressing routine say the nursery rhyme These Are Baby's Fingers, listed above.

MY BABY WILL – Look up at my face and make eye contact. They may kick, wiggle or make sounds to show pleasure.

THEN I WILL – Use tone of voice and facial expressions to keep my baby's attention as I dress them and say the nursery rhyme.

TIP

Try and incorporate your baby's name into the rhyme instead of using the word baby.

WEEK 10: COZY CHATS – LISTEN FOR THE COO

AREA ADDRESSED – Expressive Language

SKILL TARGETED – Makes cooing noises for pleasure

WHY DO THIS? – One of the earliest speech and language milestones a baby hits in their journey to first words is cooing. Cooing occurs most often when infants are feeling relaxed and playful and engaged in pleasurable interactions with an adult. When a parent responds back to their infant's coos, they are teaching their baby the sounds they make are important and have an effect on the listener, as well as providing their first experience of vocal turn-taking in a social interaction with another person.

THINGS YOU NEED – Yourself and baby

SPECIAL THINGS TO REMEMBER – Coos sound like soft, drawn-out vowels, such as "ooooooo" or "aaaaaaa", maybe even "gooooooo" or "gaaaaa".

ACTIVITY – Get into a comfortable position, like snuggling up on the bed or sofa, and come face-to-face with your baby. Start talking to your baby about whatever comes naturally to you. You could talk about what happened that day or just how much you love them. Take 5-10 second pauses in between sentences to give your baby lots of space to add their own voice into the "conversation".

MY BABY WILL – Gaze at my face and make cooing noises as we talk.

THEN I WILL – Smile at my baby and imitate the noises they have made to encourage them to make them again. Continue the "conversation" for as long as my baby is happy to do so.

TIP

This activity may take some practice before you and your baby establish a real back-and-forth "conversation". Choose a time in your daily routine where you can snuggle up for these language-boosting cozy chats for at least five minutes every day.

WEEK 11: SOUNDS AROUND – A LISTENING GAME

AREA ADDRESSED – Phonological Development

SKILL TARGETED – Responds to environmental sounds

WHY DO THIS? – As your baby learns to talk over the next year, it is not only valuable for them to hear speech, but to hear all the other sounds around them in the environment. A healthy listening experience is critical for babies to begin to figure out which sounds are important for speaking and which are not, as well as to enrich their developing auditory system.

> Monitoring your baby's hearing throughout their early years is critical to healthy speech and language development. Talk to your doctor right away if you ever have questions or concerns about your baby's hearing.

THINGS YOU NEED - Yourself, baby, stroller or carrier

SPECIAL THINGS TO REMEMBER – Noises that are too loud may frighten your baby or in extreme cases may damage their hearing. Rule of thumb: if it is too loud for you it is definitely too loud for your baby. Aim for volumes no higher than normal speaking level.

ACTIVITY – Take your baby out for a walk. Notice all the sounds in the environment as you and your baby walk. Go slowly, pausing to let your baby hear these sounds too. Sounds you may notice are:
- traffic noises
- animal sounds
- sounds of nature (e.g., wind blowing in trees)
- footsteps on the ground
- other people in the environment

MY BABY WILL – Look around and listen to sounds as we walk.

THEN I WILL – Talk about the sounds I am hearing with my baby using infant-directed speech.

TIP

Remember talking to your baby is great but it is not the only thing for them to listen to. It is important to offer lots of other listening experiences too. Use the suggestions provided in this book (p.28) to let your baby listen to other noises around them this week.

WEEK 12: LITTLE LIP READER

AREA ADDRESSED – Phonological Development

SKILL TARGETED – Learning the speech sounds in language

WHY DO THIS? – Babies love to watch our mouths move as we talk. In fact, studies have shown that very young infants are trying to figure out which sounds come out depending on what our mouths look like. By offering babies more opportunities to watch our mouths and listen to the sounds that come out when we talk, we are providing their developing brain with more linguistic input for them to use to try and figure out just how to make these sounds themselves.

THINGS YOU NEED - Yourself, baby, stroller

SPECIAL THINGS TO REMEMBER – There are many moments in the day when you and your baby naturally come face-to-face. Being aware of how to capitalize on these moments, by allowing a few extra seconds to let your baby watch your mouth while you talk to them, is another easy way to add language boosting talking time into your daily routine.

ACTIVITY – After putting your baby in the stroller, stop and remain face-to-face. Take a few seconds to let your baby focus on your face or direct their attention to look at you with your voice. Talk to them about where you are going and what will happen when you get there and let them watch your mouth as you speak.

MY BABY WILL – Focus their attention on my face, including watching my lips move as I speak.

THEN I WILL – Try and keep my baby's attention by using infant-directed speech as I talk.

TIP

Use other times when you come naturally face-to-face with your baby for even more talking time, such as diaper change, dressing, feeding, bathing, putting them in and out of car seats, while in forward facing carriers and while rocking or cuddling them.

OTHER ENVIRONMENTAL NOISES

Around the house:
- doorbell
- alarm clock or radio
- water running
- knock on the door
- mobile music
- cupboards opening and closing
- rain on the window

On a walk:
- birds chirping
- wind in the trees
- dog barking
- car horns
- traffic driving by
- footsteps on the ground

In the car:
- door opening and closing
- music on the radio
- buckles snapping
- buttons pushing
- people getting in and out

Toys:
- small musical instruments
- soft toys that make a noise
- noisy books
- music from baby rockers/seats
- rattles and shakers

NURSERY RHYMES

HICKORY DICKORY DOCK	**HUMPTY DUMPTY**
Hickory, dickory dock. The mouse ran up the clock. The clock struck one, The mouse ran down, Hickory, dickory dock.	Humpty dumpty sat on a wall, Humpty Dumpty had a great fall. All the kings horses and all the kings men, Couldn't put Humpty together again.
PAT-A-CAKE	**JACK AND JILL WENT UP THE HILL**
Pat-a-cake, pat-a-cake, baker man. Bake me a cake as fast as you can. Roll it, pat it, mark it with a 'B', And put it in the oven for Baby and me!	Jack and Jill, Went up the hill, To fetch a pail of water. Jack fell down, And broke his crown, And Jill came tumbling after.

3 MONTHS OLD

WEEK 13: SINGING FOR SOUNDS – A VOWEL ENCOURAGEMENT GAME

AREA ADDRESSED – Expressive Language

SKILL TARGETED – Uses a variety of different vowel sounds in vocalizations

WHY DO THIS? – At this age your baby is trying to gain more control over their own voice and singing songs is an easy and fun way to encourage them to do so. Giving your baby opportunities to make different sounds lets them practice becoming purposeful with their voice, which is another important step in helping them learn to talk.

THINGS YOU NEED – Yourself and baby

SPECIAL THINGS TO REMEMBER – Sing these songs a few times each day so your baby is familiar with the routine of the actions and the language. The more familiar the song is, the more likely your baby will be to add in their own voice. Some babies may like to listen to the song lying down and looking up at you and some may prefer being bounced on your knee. Find what works best to encourage your baby to use their voice and go with it!

> ### Wheels On The Bus
>
> The wheels on the bus go round and round, round and round, round and round.
> The wheels on the bus go round and round, all through the town.
> (Circle baby's legs around while singing this verse.)
>
> The horn on the bus goes beep, beep, beep.
> (Tickle baby's tummy when you sing "beep"),
> The people on the bus go up and down.
> (Raise up/down baby's arms or pick baby up/down as you sing).

ACTIVITY – Sing the song and add actions that your baby might enjoy. For example, when the "people go up and down" bounce your baby on your knee or lift them up in the air. Pause for 5-10 seconds during the parts of the song you think your baby enjoys the most to give them a chance to add their own voice in too.

MY BABY WILL – Make vowel-like sounds during the song that sound like "aaaaaa", "oooooooo" or "eeeeeeeee".

THEN I WILL – Imitate my baby's sounds and smile at them. Then continue with the song for as long as my baby is happy to do so.

TIP

Try posting a song list up where you can see it each day as a reminder to incorporate singing into your daily routine.

WEEK 14: BRINGING OUT THE SOCIAL SMILE

AREA ADDRESSED – Pragmatic/Social Language

SKILL TARGETED – Smiles to signal pleasure

WHY DO THIS? – Smiling in response to what another person says or does is a very social and uniquely human thing to do. Around 2 or 3 months of age, babies begin to reach this major milestone in communication and start to try and match the timing of their smiling with an adult. Research shows that when parents engage infants in games that elicit back-and-forth smiling, babies start to become more sophisticated at coordinating these social interactions. These small but important games are a first step in learning that communication isn't just about words, but the purposeful and successful coordination of interactions with another person.

THINGS YOU NEED – Yourself and baby

SPECIAL THINGS TO REMEMBER – Every baby is different. Something that makes one baby smile could make another break into tears. Use all the clues you have learned from your baby over the last few months to help determine what might make them smile, then add lots of these ideas into your day!

ACTIVITY – Get into a comfortable position with your baby and come face-to-face. Smile at your baby! Tell them you are ready to play a game together and choose one of the activities below to try and encourage your baby to smile.

- Recite a favourite nursery rhyme
- Make funny faces
- Tickles
- Making silly noises

MY BABY WILL – Know it is time to play when I come down face-to-face. They may gaze up at me or even smile first before I start to play the game.

THEN I WILL – Smile in return and start the game. While we play, I will make sure to leave pauses to give my baby a chance to smile and signal they are excited. I will repeat the activity for as long as my baby is happy to do so.

TIP

Talk to your family members about other ideas that might make your baby smile.

WEEK 15: MIRROR PEEK-A-BOO

AREA ADDRESSED – Pragmatic/Social Language

SKILL TARGETED – Imitates facial expressions

WHY DO THIS? – When responsive adults play imitation games with infants it provides them with an opportunity to practice the back-and-forth exchanges that occur during learning. At a basic level you are teaching your baby the routine of first watching another person, then trying to repeat that behaviour themselves. This is a skill they will need to master over the course of the next few years as they learn to repeat sounds, words and sentences. On a larger level you are teaching them that there is a relationship between what someone is thinking and what they are doing, and in turn, how their own simple actions can have an effect on another person.

THINGS YOU NEED – Yourself, baby, a mirror

SPECIAL THINGS TO REMEMBER – The key to this activity being successful is to give your baby lots of practice to understand the game of imitation. By adding this quick activity consistently into your daily bath routine your baby will soon learn to watch your face and try to imitate your silly and fun expressions.

ACTIVITY – Before bath time, pick up your baby and bring them in front of the mirror. Let them look at you and look at themselves, then step to the side so you are no longer in front of the mirror. Wait a few seconds then step in front of the mirror again and make an exaggerated surprised face with your mouth wide open. Hold for 3-5 seconds. Let your baby see your face then say, "Hello (use your baby's name)!" in an excited tone. Repeat 5-10 times or for as long as your baby wants to play this game.

MY BABY WILL – Watch my face in the mirror and attempt to open up their mouth to copy my facial expression.

THEN I WILL – Smile at my baby and tell them they are such a good "copycat". Tell them you are going to play again and repeat the activity.

TIP

Once your baby is doing well imitating you, see if they can imitate other family members too.

WEEK 16: FUNNY FINGER PLAYS – WATCH WITH ME

AREA ADDRESSED – Communication Development

SKILL TARGETED – Joint attention

WHY DO THIS? – Joint attention is when two people are looking at the same thing, at the same time. Babies develop this skill from birth to 18 months of age and it is one of the most important early skills to learn for a healthy language development. Research shows that when parents engage their infants in more joint attention activities while their children are under 18 months of age, these babies go on to develop stronger vocabulary skills as toddlers.

THINGS YOU NEED – Yourself and baby

SPECIAL THINGS TO REMEMBER – Your baby is just starting to learn how to focus on objects other than an adult's face. That is to say, they are at the very beginning of developing joint attention skills; so when you move your fingers during the rhyme, go slowly. Give your baby lots of time to turn their head or move their eyes to follow your fingers as they dance across their line of vision.

ACTIVITY – Try the finger play song Beehive when your baby is in the quiet alert phase and ready to play. Come face-to-face with your baby before you begin and hold your hands about 30-40 centimeters from their face.

MY BABY WILL – Watch my fingers as I say the rhyme and track them with their eyes as I move them across their line of sight.

THEN I WILL – Go slowly as I move my fingers in front of my baby's face so we can have a chance to focus on them together as they pass by. I will entice my baby to watch my finger pass across their line of sight by wiggling it around as I "fly" the bee from the "beehive".

Beehive

Here is the beehive but where are the bees?
(Make a fist and shake it gently for your baby to see.)
Hidden away where nobody sees.
(Pretend to look inside your fist then look back at baby.)
Open it up and out they fly.
(Open your fist.)
One, two, three, four, five…
(Use your other hand to touch one finger at a time from your "beehive" hand as each "bee" flies across to the other side while you count – just like bees who would be coming out of the hive.)
Buzzzz!
(Tickle baby with both hands.)

TIP

Not only is this a great language building activity but is an easy "on the go" game to keep baby entertained and happy while you are out. Great times to do any finger play games include waiting in line or while sitting in restaurants.

3 MONTH MILESTONES AND MEMORIES

Congratulations! With your help your baby has completed the first part of their journey towards first words! Here is what your baby is able to do now:

	Understanding Language	Using Language
Birth to 3 Months	Startles to loud noises	Makes reflexive noises such as coughing, burping and sneezing
	Appears to recognize a parent's voice by quieting or smiling when spoken to	Smiles when interacting with a parent or caregiver
	Turns head or seems to focus in response to sounds	Cries to express various needs (e.g., hunger, fatigue, pain, etc.)
		Makes cooing noises to express pleasure

Here are all the things you're now doing each day to help them prepare to say words:

Aware of my baby's cries for different needs	Engaging my baby in imitation games	Playing games to encourage smiling from my baby
Using bath time for talking time	Making eye contact with my baby	Letting my baby see my mouth as I talk during daily face-to-face interactions
Beginning a daily story routine	Saying nursery rhymes during dressing routines	Using infant-directed speech when talking to my baby
Using lullabies to soothe my baby	Making listening time a part of our day together	Using finger plays to encourage joint attention
Reading my baby's state of arousal to help meet their needs	Encouraging my baby to use lots of sounds during cozy chats, songs and play	Talking to other family members about my baby's language development

3 MONTH MILESTONES AND MEMORIES

PUT A PICTURE OF YOUR BABY HERE

What was your baby's favourite thing to do with you in these early months?
_____
_____
_____
_____
_____

What did your baby like the least?
_____
_____
_____
_____
_____

Record a special memory from your baby's language learning journey so far.
_____
_____
_____
_____
_____

IT'S ABOUT TO GET NOISY

LEARNING TO USE THEIR VOICE

# 4 MONTHS OLD

WEEK 17: TICKLE TURNS – LISTEN FOR THE LAUGH

AREA ADDRESSED – Expressive Language

SKILL TARGETED – Laughs for pleasure during social interactions

WHY DO THIS? – When your baby reaches the milestone of laughing, it is such a special moment for both parent and child. Engaging in games that encourage your baby to laugh not only reinforces the communication connection between you both, but also lets your baby practice using another way to send you a message. Just as crying is a signal that something is wrong, a baby's laugh is a signal that something is going well and should continue.

THINGS YOU NEED – Yourself and baby

SPECIAL THINGS TO REMEMBER – Studies show that young babies look to their parents for cues when something is "funny". Use your facial expressions and voice to encourage your baby to play, have fun and laugh! Chances are the more fun you have, the more fun your baby will have too, and give you a big belly laugh.

ACTIVITY – After diaper change come face-to-face with your baby and start a very simple tickle routine. Repeat the game several times so your baby can become familiar with the routine.

    Step 1: Say, "Where is (baby's name) belly?"
    Step 2: Say, "There it is!" then give your baby tickles or kisses on their belly.

MY BABY WILL – Become excited with anticipation when I am about to tickle them. They will smile and laugh while I'm giving kisses or tickling them indicating they are having fun and want to keep playing.

THEN I WILL – Repeat the game again until my baby indicates they do not want to play anymore by looking away or fussing.

TIP

Since all babies are unique this is only one way to get a baby to laugh. Funny noises, faces or silly actions, also get giggles from little ones. Talk with your family members about other ways to encourage your baby to laugh based on what you already know about your child's unique personality. Share ideas with each other.

WEEK 18: VOCAL PLAY - LET'S GET NOISY BABY!

AREA ADDRESSED – Expressive Language

SKILL TARGETED – Engages in vocal play

WHY DO THIS? – At this age your baby is gaining confidence with their vocal abilities and is now ready to try and incorporate their lips, tongue and jaw to make new sounds. You will notice over the next few months that the variety of sounds they use increases, as well as how often they are making noises. You may also hear squeals, growls and other funny noises. There are two important reasons to encourage your baby to make all these sounds. Firstly, making these noises helps babies gain control over the parts of the body that are required to make speech sounds, such as the tongue and lips. Also, during vocal play babies begin to coordinate the movements they are making with the sound they hear come out, which is a step toward purposeful communication.

THINGS YOU NEED - Yourself, baby, blanket, different rattles

SPECIAL THINGS TO REMEMBER – Speech-language pathologists refer to this stage in language development as vocal play. Research suggests babies tend to use shorter durations of vocal play when engaged in face-to-face interactions and use longer strings of vocal noises on their own.

ACTIVITY – Place a blanket between you and your baby and let them see you hide three or four small rattles underneath. Encourage your baby to feel the top of the blanket until they touch one of the rattles. Pull that rattle out and shake it for your baby. Talk to them about what they are seeing and hearing. Pause and give them a chance to make a noise, then give the rattle to your baby. Encourage them to make noises by allowing them time to explore the rattle, talking to them and waiting. When they are ready, move on to finding the other rattles under the blanket.

MY BABY WILL – Explore the texture, sight and sound of the rattle. They may shake it or put it in their mouth. As they explore they may make vocal play noises.

THEN I WILL – Allow my baby to explore the rattle. I will smile, talk and imitate the sounds they make trying to encourage them to makes lots of different noises as we play.

TIP

You may hear your baby making vocal play noises on their own during your daily routine. Do not interrupt them! It is important for them to have these private practice sessions just as much as it is to have the vocal play sessions with you.

WEEK 19: AN EVERYDAY STORYTELLER – NARRATING DAILY ROUTINES

AREA ADDRESSED – Phonological Development

SKILL TARGETED – Hears the sounds of language

WHY DO THIS? – Although it may seem silly to talk to someone who can't yet answer back, talking to your baby is the absolute most important thing you can do to help them develop strong language skills. In fact, studies show that there is a relationship between how many words a young child hears and their language skills. Parents who exposed their babies to lots of talking during their typical daily routines were more likely to have toddlers and preschoolers with stronger language skills compared to those who spoke less often.

THINGS YOU NEED – Yourself and baby

SPECIAL THINGS TO REMEMBER – This type of activity is what speech-language pathologists refer to as self-talk. You talk out loud about what you're seeing, doing, hearing or feeling as your baby listens. This activity is a very easy way to add a little language learning in while getting a few other things done as well.

ACTIVITY – Each time you and your baby are getting ready to leave the house, use this moment to become an "everyday storyteller". Talk to your baby about what you are doing, while you are doing it.

> Example:
> "Now we're putting on your shoes. This shoe goes on this foot (while putting it on their foot), and this shoe goes on the other foot (while putting it on their foot).
> Let's get your coat (while picking up the coat). Let's put this arm in (while putting an arm in the coat sleeve) and now this arm in (while putting an arm in the coat sleeve). Now we zip it up (while zipping up the coat)."

MY BABY WILL – Watch and listen to me as I talk and get us ready to go out.

THEN I WILL – Continue to talk about what I'm doing as I'm doing it, until we are ready to leave. If my baby makes noises while I'm talking, I will pause to let them add their own voice into the "conversation". I will respond by smiling and encouraging these noises, then continue narrating and getting them ready.

TIP

Narrating can be done anywhere or anytime, so talk freely during the day because your baby is listening. Just remember to take pauses as well so your baby has a chance to add their own voice in if they choose to!

WEEK 20: OUR FIRST GAME – BABY BUBBLE PLAY

AREA ADDRESSED – Play Development

SKILL TARGETED – Engages in a back-and-forth play routine with an adult

WHY DO THIS? – Until now the play you have been doing with your baby has mainly been without objects, but by this age your baby can reach and grasp and is gaining more control over their body. That's why now is a great time to start adding more items into play to stimulate your baby's growing abilities and senses. Research indicates that even very young infants learn through play. Play increases brain development and growth and it is an important facilitator of language development. In short, the more a baby can play, the better their language skills are likely to be.

THINGS YOU NEED - Yourself, baby, bubbles

SPECIAL THINGS TO REMEMBER – At this stage play is all about stimulating a baby's senses and learning about cause and effect. Play items that are safe for your baby to touch and explore are the kinds of items to introduce into daily routines.

ACTIVITY – Place your baby in a supported sitting position, an infant seat or lay them on their back. Provide them with lots of space to move and reach. Come face-to-face with your baby and blow bubbles through the wand softly towards them.

MY BABY WILL – Watch the bubbles float around them. They may try to reach for the bubbles as they pass by overhead.

THEN I WILL – Talk to my baby about what I am seeing, doing and feeling (self-talk). I will get into a simple back-and-forth routine of blowing bubbles and then letting my baby explore. If my baby uses sounds, I will imitate the sounds they make then continue to use self-talk during the activity.

TIP

Keep the bubble container in a place where you can easily see it as a reminder to add this fun game into your daily routine for a few minutes every day.

WHEN TO ADD NARRATING INTO YOUR ROUTINE

Around the house:
- while cooking
- when getting dressed
- during diaper change routine
- while putting laundry away
- when tidying up toys
- while getting the bath ready
- while doing dishes
- when eating meals together

On the go:
- when out for a walk
- at the grocery store
- playing at the park
- getting into and out of the car
- while waiting in line

GREAT FIRST TOYS FOR YOUR BABY

Classic toys:
- soft books
- balls
- play mats or baby gyms
- mirrors (non-breakable)
- soft blocks
- rattles
- soft toys that offer a multisensory experience
- puppets
- nesting cups
- stuffed animals
- small musical instruments (drum, piano, shakers)
- pop-up toy
- activity cubes

"Toys" from around the house:
- blankets (hide things under or for peek-a-boo)
- plastic cups (roll or stack)
- wooden spoons (bang with)
- plastic containers (put things in and dump things out)
- plastic measuring spoons on a ring
- water bottle (sealed tightly) with dried beans inside for musical shaker
- DIY sock puppet

5 MONTHS OLD

WEEK 21: MOMMY/DADDY THE MIME – ADDING GESTURES TO EVERYDAY TALK

AREA ADDRESSED – Receptive Language

SKILL TARGETED – Understands meaning of familiar words

WHY DO THIS? – By now your baby has become familiar with lots of different speech sounds and their brain is starting to pick up patterns for which sounds may go together to form words. Once their brain has identified a grouping of sounds they think is a word, the next step is to figure out what that word might mean. Babies try to figure out word meanings by using clues from their environment and one clue babies are very sensitive to is gesture use. Studies show that infants whose parents used more gestures to communicate with them during their first few years of life, had larger vocabularies as toddlers and at school age.

THINGS YOU NEED – Yourself and baby

SPECIAL THINGS TO REMEMBER – Remembering to use gestures when speaking to your baby takes practice, so really try to commit to using gestures in at least one daily routine each day. This will go a long way to helping you pick up the habit and pretty soon you will be using this language boosting strategy all day long without even realizing it.

ACTIVITY – Sit your baby somewhere they can see you during mealtime (e.g., highchair, infant seat, etc.). Place items needed for your meal on the table, out of your baby's reach, but in their view. Use gestures to describe each item to your baby as you eat. Here's an example:

> "Now it's lunch time. I have an apple today (hold up the apple).
> Looks good. I'm going to take a bite (bite the apple). Yum yum!
> Here is my sandwich (point to the sandwich). Time to eat my sandwich (take a bite of the sandwich).
> Where is my cup? Oh there is my cup (point to the cup)! Now I need a big drink from my cup (take a drink)."

MY BABY WILL - Listen to my words and watch me as I talk and use gestures to support what I am saying. They may even use vocal play sounds and/or reach out to touch and explore what I am showing them or talking about.

THEN I WILL - Continue to use gestures throughout my meal as I talk to my baby. If feasible and safe, I will let them touch and explore items they have reached for.

TIP

This is a great way to start introducing your baby to a family mealtime routine since they will be getting ready to start eating their own solid foods in the coming weeks!

WEEK 22: OWN NAME HIDE AND SEEK

AREA ADDRESSED – Receptive Language

SKILL TARGETED – Responds to their own name

WHY DO THIS? – Babies begin to understand words months before they actually say a word for the first time. One of the first words a baby understands is their own name. With continued practice of hearing their name, babies learn to respond appropriately to hearing this word (e.g., looking at who has said their name) and it is the very beginning of building their early vocabularies.

THINGS YOU NEED – Yourself and baby

SPECIAL THINGS TO REMEMBER – Play this game in different rooms in the house. Try hiding in a variety of different positions around your baby to encourage them to turn their head and try to look toward where they heard their name being called.

ACTIVITY – Have your baby in a supported sitting position or lay them down on their tummy. Tell them you are going to hide and they have to find you. Then hide out of your baby's view, wait for a few seconds, and call their name.

MY BABY WILL - Look up and in the direction of where their name was called.

THEN I WILL - Pop out from my hiding place and say, "You found me!" and give my baby lots of hugs and tickles. I will repeat the game for as long as my baby is happy to play.

TIP

Invite other family members to play this game too, and once your baby can crawl, encourage them to come and find you!

WEEK 23: YOU REACH, THEN I TEACH – IN PLAY

AREA ADDRESSED – Receptive Language

SKILL TARGETED – Recognizes familiar words

WHY DO THIS? – In the previous months you were the leader in play; choosing what items to offer your baby while they watched you. Now that your baby is moving and reaching more, it's time to let them become the leader in your interactions. It is now your turn to watch their body and decide what they are interested in, either by what they are looking at or reaching for, then talk about that object. Research indicates that parents who respond to their baby's preverbal noises (e.g., coos, babbles, vocal play) and intentions in play, by talking about what they are looking at or doing, have babies who develop words faster.

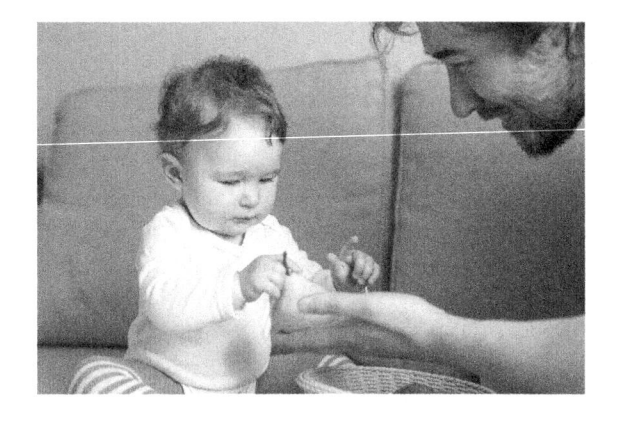

THINGS YOU NEED - Yourself, baby, toys or household items, a basket

SPECIAL THINGS TO REMEMBER – Give your baby lots of time to look, engage and maybe reach for an item that interests them before jumping in. Let them be the leader of the game. Keep the basket of items easily accessible so you can play this game whenever you and your baby are ready each day.

ACTIVITY – Place your baby in a supported sitting position then sit across from them. Have five to ten items in a basket that stimulate a variety of your baby's senses (e.g., make noise, are shiny, light up, have a variety of textures, etc.). You can use toys or items from around the house. See an example list provided at the end of this chapter (p.53). Bring the basket close to your baby and encourage them to take out an item.

MY BABY WILL - Look in the basket and reach in to grab an item. They may use vocal play or babble as they explore the object.

THEN I WILL – Talk to my baby about what they have reached for. I will tell them what the object is and describe what they see, hear and feel. I will try to use infant-directed speech as I talk.

TIP

This game can be done around the house or on the go. Whenever you give your baby a chance to reach, you can teach! Simply talk about what they are interested in.

WEEK 24: LET'S PLAY BALL – A TURN-TAKING GAME

AREA ADDRESSED – Pragmatic/Social Language

SKILL TARGETED – Plays turn-taking games with an adult

WHY DO THIS? – In order for a baby to become a confident communicator they have to learn some basic skills, such as how to take turns in conversations. Infants begin learning about turn-taking during simple, familiar play routines starting at around 5 months of age. Over the next several months, the more opportunities your baby has to participate in these back-and-forth play routines with you, the stronger their turn-taking skills become. Research shows that babies who participate in lots of turn-taking activities during the first two years of their lives tend to have stronger communication abilities by preschool age.

THINGS YOU NEED - Yourself, baby, a ball

SPECIAL THINGS TO REMEMBER – Keep in mind, your baby is just starting to learn to play with objects and take turns, so repeating this activity daily will be helpful. The aim is to establish a back-and-forth turn-taking game your baby enjoys to play with you.

ACTIVITY – Place your baby in a supported sitting position. Sit across from your baby and tell them you are going to play ball together. Give your baby the ball and let them explore it. Then encourage them to push it or roll it to you, either with your facial expressions, words or by gently physically prompting them to do so.

MY BABY WILL - Push/roll the ball in my direction, either on their own or with support.

THEN I WILL - Smile and cheer for them as I catch the ball. When I have the ball I will use this as my cue to talk (e.g., "Ok mommy has the ball now. This is a big ball!"). I will then roll the ball back to my baby slowly. When my baby has the ball I will pause, giving them a chance to use their own voice to babble or make noises if they choose to. I will continue this way, trying to establish a simple back-and-forth routine using the ball as a guide.

TIP

An inflatable beach ball is a great first ball to use with babies. It is light and large making it very easy for your baby to push it towards you on their own.

EXAMPLES OF DAILY ROUTINES WITH GESTURES

During dressing routine, say:
"Here is your shirt (hold up the shirt).
Let's put it on (while putting it on your baby).
Here is one sock (while holding up a sock) and the other sock (while holding up the other sock).
Let's put them on (while putting the socks on)."

During bath time, say:
"Time to go in the bath (while pointing to the tub).
Now let's wash your arm (pointing to your baby's arm).
Now let's wash your foot. Where is that foot? There it is (point to their foot)!"

During diaper change routine, say:
"Time to put your diaper on (hold up the diaper).
Let's lift you up (while raising your baby's bottom).
Then put the diaper under you (while putting the diaper under your baby).
And do it all up (while securing the diaper)!"

YOU REACH, THEN I TEACH ACTIVITY

Items that might be included:
- different textured fabrics (cloths, small blankets, etc.)
- baby clothes
- small pillows with different colours and patterns
- brushes and combs
- balls
- small toys
- plastic cups
- small family picture albums
- sponges
- small shoes
- ribbon
- rattles
- blocks
- any toy or item from around the house that is safe for your baby to touch and explore!

6 MONTHS OLD

WEEK 25: COPY ME – THE MUSICAL KITCHEN

AREA ADDRESSED – Pragmatic/Social Language

SKILL TARGETED – Imitates simple actions

WHY DO THIS? – There are two important reasons to engage babies at this age in imitation activities. Firstly, to help them learn something about an object or an action being demonstrated. And secondly, to develop the social function of imitation, where a baby learns about coordinating interactions with another person. Babies develop the skill of imitation from birth through the first few years of life as they learn more and more about becoming part of the world of communication.

> **My Musical Kitchen**
>
> *To the tune of The Wheels On The Bus.*
> *Each time you say "bang", hit the pot.*
>
> The pots in the kitchen go,
> Bang, bang, bang.
> Bang, bang, bang. Bang, bang, bang.
> The pots in the kitchen go,
> Bang, bang, bang.
> All morning long!

THINGS YOU NEED - Yourself, baby, pots, wooden spoons

SPECIAL THINGS TO REMEMBER – Babies love simple cause and effect activities so this should be a game they really enjoy, but as always, the more fun you have, the more likely your baby will be to join in and have fun too!

ACTIVITY – Sit across from your baby on the floor. Put out three pots, turned upside down between you and your baby. Give both you and your baby a wooden spoon then tell your baby you are going to sing the My Musical Kitchen Song and that they should copy you. Bang on one of the pots a few times to show your baby the action you want them to imitate. Begin singing to engage your baby in play.

MY BABY WILL - Bang the pot with the wooden spoon at any time during the song.

THEN I WILL - Use facial expressions and words to encourage my baby to imitate my actions. I will leave a 5-10 second pause between versus of the song as a signal to my baby that it is their turn to participate by banging the pot. If my baby does not imitate my actions after singing the song three times I will gently guide their hand and prompt them to imitate me.

TIP

Babies remember imitation tasks up to one or two days later if they are done in the same place with the same things, so try and keep the setting and materials consistent as you practice this imitation game with your baby this week.

WEEK 26: COPY ME – THE BATH TIME BABBLE BOX

AREA ADDRESSED – Expressive Language

SKILL TARGETED – Engages in babbling with a variety of sounds

WHY DO THIS? – Babbling is one of the major milestones in speech development. Infants who only use a few sounds in their babbling, those who do not babble often, or those that develop babbling late, are at risk of later delays in speech and language development as toddlers. Giving your baby lots of opportunities to practice babbling is part of a healthy language development. In fact, research shows that infants are listening to a parent's responses to their babbling and use this information to help them learn how to make more sounds.

THINGS YOU NEED - Yourself, baby, box with a variety of household items or toys

SPECIAL THINGS TO REMEMBER – Babbling develops from 6-9 months old. Babbling is different from vocal play because a baby will start repeating true syllables over and over (e.g. babababa or wowowowo).

ACTIVITY – Place five to seven household items that are safe for your baby to explore, or some small toys that are waterproof, into a box. Make sure each item in the box starts with a different speech sound that your baby will use during the babbling phase. Keep this box by the bathtub. When bath time begins, encourage your baby to choose a toy or item from the box. As they explore the toy, model the speech sound associated with that object during play. You can do this by making noises or using words. Repeat the specific sounds or words over and over as you and your baby play with that item. See an example list at the end of the chapter on p.61 for ideas.

MY BABY WILL - Explore the toy and make babbling sounds. They may imitate the sounds I am using or use their own sounds.

THEN I WILL - Imitate the sounds my baby has made. I will use my facial expressions and voice to encourage my baby to make the sound again. When it seems like my baby has had enough of that toy I will let them choose another one from the box.

TIP

Some babies are more vocal than others, and this is normal. Remember to leave lots of pauses as you talk and play to give your baby a chance to use their own voice too.

WEEK 27: YOU REACH, THEN I TEACH – WITH BOOKS

AREA ADDRESSED – Early Literacy

SKILL TARGETED – Enjoys reading with an adult

WHY DO THIS? – By this age the way you read to your baby needs to start to change. Your baby is no longer laying passively listening to your voice. They are sitting up, looking at pictures and even reaching to interact with the book. Research tells us that it is important to keep a child's motives and interests in mind during shared storybook reading even early on, for example by choosing books based on a baby's preferences and talking to them about what interests them on the page. This makes the interaction more pleasant and engaging for the child, making it more likely that they will develop a positive attitude towards book reading. In fact, children who participated in positive shared book reading experiences early on tended to be more likely to read books at four and five years old, compared to those who began shared book reading when they were older.

THINGS YOU NEED – Yourself, baby, books

SPECIAL THINGS TO REMEMBER – Books that offer a multisensory experience (e.g., light up, have a variety of textures, make noises, bright colours, etc.) are ideal to engage babies in book reading for longer periods.

ACTIVITY – Sit in a comfortable position with your baby. Open the book and watch where your baby looks and/or reaches, then talk about this item on the page. As you move along in the book you can choose to read the words on the page, or simply talk about what your baby is interested in; whatever works best for you and your baby.

MY BABY WILL - Put their hand somewhere on the page of the book and/or look at something in particular on the page.

THEN I WILL - Point to that image and talk about what we are seeing, hearing or feeling. I will encourage my baby to explore the book by responding positively each time they reach out, and pausing to look and talk about what interests them on the page at that moment.

TIP

At this age babies love to explore books with their eyes, fingers and their mouth. This is all normal! If you have a baby that loves to chew, try keeping teethers nearby so you can easily offer them something to chew on instead of the book.

WEEK 28: TAKE THE QUIZ – WHAT I HAVE LEARNED SO FAR

WHY DO THIS? – Supporting your baby's early language development requires reliable information. Knowing you have accurate knowledge is the first step to ensure their healthy development.

SPECIAL THINGS TO REMEMBER – Your child has so many people that love them! Share this quiz with them so you can all learn together.

Take the quiz
Answer true or false to the statements below:

1) Reading to babies before they can talk is silly because it has no effect on their language and literacy development.

2) Using baby talk (or infant-directed speech) with a baby will harm their overall language development.

3) Cooing is when babies make long, vowel-like sounds and is one of the earliest vocal development milestones, occurring between 2-3 months of age.

4) When my baby becomes very loud, screeching and making nonsense noises, I should always quiet them down.

5) One of the first words a baby understands is their own name at around 5-6 months old.

6) Playing turn-taking games with infants, like rolling a ball back-and-forth or popping bubbles, (blow-pop, blow-pop, etc.) has nothing to do with language development.

7) My baby will learn language best if I talk all day, all the time.

8) Encouraging my baby to imitate my facial expressions, actions and sounds will help with the development of their language skills.

9) Joint attention is when two people are looking at the same thing, at the same time and is an important skill for a baby to develop during their early years for healthy language development.

10) Babbling is when a baby repeats the same consonant-vowel sound (e.g., bababab) and a lack of babbling, delayed babbling or minimal babbling, are risk factors for later speech and language delays.

Answers: 1) F 2) F 3) T 4) F 5) T 6) F 7) F 8) T 9) T 10) T

IMITATION ACTIVITIES

Other ideas to try with your baby:
- throw a ball
- push large buttons on pop-up toys
- pull a blanket off from covering your face in peek-a-boo
- hug dolls or teddies
- shake rattles, maracas or bells
- bang a drum
- push piano keys
- push a cupboard door closed
- open a book
- push a block tower over
- bang plastic cups together
- pour water from containers during bath time

BATH TIME BABBLE BOX IDEAS

These are a few ideas to get you started! Be creative and come up with your own based on your baby's interests.

Speech Sound	Objects/Toys	Noises Or Words To Use
w	<ul><li>fire truck</li><li>airplane</li><li>dog</li></ul>	<ul><li>wee ooh, wee ooh!</li><li>whoosh!</li><li>woof woof</li></ul>
y	<ul><li>toy food</li><li>ball</li><li>cloth</li></ul>	<ul><li>yum yum</li><li>yeah!</li><li>wash your ….</li></ul>
m	<ul><li>cow</li><li>cat</li><li>spoon</li></ul>	<ul><li>moo</li><li>meow</li><li>mix mix</li></ul>
n	<ul><li>horse</li><li>doll</li><li>items that sink</li></ul>	<ul><li>neigh neigh</li><li>knee, nose or night-night</li><li>oh no!</li></ul>
b	<ul><li>truck or car</li><li>bowl</li><li>sheep</li></ul>	<ul><li>beep beep</li><li>bowl or bang</li><li>baa baa</li></ul>
p	<ul><li>animals</li><li>bubbles</li><li>cup</li></ul>	<ul><li>pat pat</li><li>pop</li><li>pour</li></ul>
t	<ul><li>train</li><li>empty container</li><li>tractor</li></ul>	<ul><li>train or toot toot</li><li>tip or tap</li><li>tractor or tuh tuh tuh!</li></ul>
d	<ul><li>duck</li><li>bucket</li><li>items that sink</li></ul>	<ul><li>duck</li><li>dump</li><li>down</li></ul>
k	<ul><li>cup</li><li>comb</li><li>keys</li></ul>	<ul><li>cup</li><li>comb</li><li>keys or click click</li></ul>
g	<ul><li>vehicles</li><li>animals</li><li>cloth</li></ul>	<ul><li>go go!</li><li>grrr!</li><li>cover things and say gone</li></ul>

GREAT FIRST BOOKS

Books With Repetition
- *Brown Bear, Brown Bear* by Bill Martin Jr.
- *Counting Kisses* by Karen Katz
- *Goodnight Moon* by Margaret Wise Brown
- *Hand, Hand, Finger, Thumb* by Al Perkins
- *Hop on Pop* by Dr. Seuss

Books With Bright Colours and Pictures
- *Can You Find Me?* by Roger Priddy
- *First 100 Words* by Priddy Bicknell Books
- *From Head To Toe* by Eric Carle
- *Where is Baby's Belly Button?* by Karen Katz
- *Where is the Green Sheep?* by Mem Fox & Judy Horacek

Books That Provide A Multisensory Experience
- *Dear Zoo* by Rod Campbell
- *Noisy Trucks* by Little Tiger Press
- *Tails* by Mathew Van Fleet
- *That's Not My Penguin* by Usborne Touchy Feely Books
- *Where's Spot?* by Eric Hill

Books With Rhythm, Rhyme and Songs
- *Five Little Monkeys* by Eileen Christelow
- *Mr. Brown Can Moo* by Dr. Seuss
- *Nursery Rhyme Picture Book* by Usborne
- *Ten in the Bed* by Kim Mitzo Thompson & Karen Mitzo Hilderbrand
- *The Wheels on the Bus* by Stephen Holmes

Wordless Picture Books
- *A Boy, A Dog and A Frog* by Mercer Mayer
- *Good Dog, Carl* by Alexandra Day
- *Goodnight Gorilla* by Peggy Rathmann
- *Have You Seen My Duckling?* by Nancy Tafuri
- *Red Sled* by Lita Judge

6 MONTH MILESTONES AND MEMORIES

Wow! Your baby is halfway to their first birthday and even closer to saying their first word! With your help, here are all the things your baby has learned to do:

	Understanding Language	**Using Language**
3 to 6 Months	Looks in the direction of sounds	Giggles and laughs for pleasure
	Watches your face while you talk to them	Uses vocalizations to express contentment or unhappiness
	Responds to changes in tone of voice	Engages in vocal play (e.g., squeals, shrieks, raspberries, etc.)
	Pays attention to melody and music	Takes turns vocalizing with an adult
		Imitates facial expressions

Here are all the new things you're doing each day to help them prepare to say words:

Engaging my baby in social interactions to make them laugh	Encouraging vocal play when my baby is alone or with me	Narrating daily routines for my baby to hear
Playing simple games with familiar routines	Using gestures as I talk to my baby	Teaching my baby to respond to their name through games
Using my baby's interests and gestures to guide interactions in play	Playing turn-taking games together	Encouraging my baby to imitate actions with objects
Encouraging different babbling sounds	Developing a love of reading by using my baby's interests to guide shared storybook reading	Gaining knowledge of typical language development and dispelling myths

6 MONTH MILESTONES AND MEMORIES

PUT A PICTURE OF YOUR BABY HERE

What speech sounds have you heard your baby use so far (w, y, m, n, p, b, d, t, k, g)?
_____
_____
_____
_____
_____

What is your baby's unique personality like; social, quiet, risk-taker? Describe some things your baby likes to do that highlight their communication style.
_____
_____
_____
_____
_____

Record something special that happened in your baby's language learning journey over the last few months.
_____
_____
_____
_____
_____

LEARNING THE MEANING OF WORDS

7 MONTHS OLD

WEEK 29: TIDY UP TIME – INCREASING THE DAILY DOSE OF SONGS

AREA ADDRESSED – Receptive Language

SKILL TARGETED – Recognizes familiar words

WHY DO THIS? – Every time you talk to your baby their brain is using different strategies to try and learn which speech sounds go together to make the words. One strategy infants use to recognize words is listening to the natural stress patterns in language that occur as we talk. When we sing, these natural stress patterns are highlighted even more, making finding words in sentences easier for babies.

> **Tidy Up Song**
>
> *To the tune of the Hi Ho The Dairy-O.*
>
> It's time to tidy up. It's time to tidy up.
> Hi, ho the dairy-o, it's time to tidy up.
> We put the toys away. We put the toys away.
> Hi, ho the dairy-o, we put the toys away.
> We pick up all the books. We pick up all the books.
> Hi, ho the dairy-o, we pick up all the books.

THINGS YOU NEED – Yourself, baby, household items or toys

SPECIAL THINGS TO REMEMBER – Infants at this age don't understand the meaning of words, so they hear all the speech sounds like one continuous string as we talk to them (e.g., "mommylovesyoumylittleboy"). The melody of songs helps babies' brains identify which sounds go together to make words by giving them clues to where words start and stop (e.g., "mommy loves you my little boy"). Once a baby discovers which sounds go together to make a word, they can then start to figure out what that word might mean. This is a critical first step in developing early vocabularies.

ACTIVITY – At the end of the day, bring your baby into a room in the house that needs to be tidied up. Start to put items away and sing while your baby watches you. You can sing the Tidy Up Song that is shown above, or try a different song that suits your baby's tastes.

MY BABY WILL - Look at me while I sing and clean up the items in the room. They may even babble or make noises too. They may crawl and pick up items around the room to try and join in.

THEN I WILL - Pause when my baby adds in their own sounds during the song so they can hear themselves. Smile and encourage this behaviour then continue singing. I will also encourage my baby to participate with me where they can by putting things in bins or picking things up.

TIP

Accompany the words in the songs with appropriate gestures and actions for an extra language boost.

WEEK 30: THE DISCOVERY DRAWER – USING PARALLEL TALK

AREA ADDRESSED – Receptive Language

SKILL TARGETED – Learning meaning for familiar words

WHY DO THIS? – Babies begin to learn the meaning of words through the interactions they have with adults in their lives each day. At this age, they do this by associating words they hear with what they are seeing or doing at the time. The more opportunity an infant has to match the spoken word they hear with the object they are seeing, or action they are doing, the easier it will be for them to learn that word meaning.

THINGS YOU NEED – Yourself, baby, household items or toys

SPECIAL THINGS TO REMEMBER – Parallel talk is a language stimulation technique that refers to having an adult talk about what a child is seeing, hearing, feeling or experiencing. The child is not required to make any verbal response back.

ACTIVITY – Place a variety of 10-15 small items you think your baby would enjoy to explore into a low drawer or cupboard in the kitchen. Multisensory items are best because they're more interesting for your baby and offer you more to talk about. Make sure everything that is in the drawer or cupboard is something your baby will be able to touch so they can explore freely and safely. They will quickly learn that this is their special place and go to it often. You can even name it after your baby (e.g., Timmy's Drawer) to personalize it for them. When you are about to make dinner take your baby into the kitchen with you. While you make dinner encourage your baby to reach into the drawer or cupboard and take out items. Look at the list on p.73 for ideas on what to add to the drawer.

MY BABY WILL - Take out an item and look at it, then explore it with their hands and mouth.

THEN I WILL - Label the item they have taken out. I will use parallel talk and tell my baby what they are seeing, hearing, or feeling as they explore the item, repeating the item name often. When you think your baby has finished exploring that item encourage them to find another one. Repeat the activity until your baby signals they no longer want to play the game.

TIP

Change items every two weeks to keep it interesting and expose your baby to new vocabulary regularly.

WEEK 31: YOU'RE THE BOSS – REVERSE IMITATION

AREA ADDRESSED – Expressive Language

SKILL TARGETED – Uses a variety of babbling sounds

WHY DO THIS? – There are many different ways an adult can respond to a baby's early babbling sounds, but imitation is the best way to get them babbling more. When an adult imitates the babbling noises a baby makes, while smiling and making eye contact with them, babies tend to make more babbling noises back! The more a baby can practice making lots of different sounds as they babble, the better it is for their language development.

THINGS YOU NEED – Yourself, baby, household items or toys

SPECIAL THINGS TO REMEMBER – Don't be discouraged if your baby doesn't make lots of noises right away. Just remember to be quiet, wait, and give them lots of time to work up to adding some of their own sounds into play.

ACTIVITY – Lay out a variety of toys on the floor that your baby typically likes to play with. These can be items from around the house or toys. Anything your baby would like to explore that comes in a pair (e.g., two balls, two rattles, two squeaky toys, etc.). Have no more than five items, and their pairs, available to play with at one time. Begin by engaging your baby in the activity; showing them what a few items can do to spark their interest. Once your baby becomes engaged with an object, you pick up its pair. Now your baby is the boss! Your job is to imitate what your baby does during play, as well as what they say. You can also use your facial expressions and silly sounds or words to make the play more fun and keep your baby interacting with you longer.

MY BABY WILL - Make some babbling sounds or other vocal noises during play. They will explore the objects in a variety of unique ways.

THEN I WILL - Imitate what my baby does with an object. I will also add some fun sounds or words to go with the actions they do. When my baby babbles I will imitate what they have said then provide a short sentence describing what they are seeing, hearing or doing (parallel talk).

TIP

This is meant to be silly and fun! When you play with your baby their way, and are excited about what they are interested in, it encourages them to play with you longer.

WEEK 32: BABY ART – A VESSEL FOR VOCABULARY

AREA ADDRESSED – Receptive Language

SKILL TARGETED – Learns meaning for familiar words

WHY DO THIS? – The types of words parents use in their everyday interactions with babies can have short and long-term benefits for a baby's growing language skills. Young infants and toddlers who are exposed to a wide variety of words tend to have stronger vocabularies. Weekly open-ended, creative activities are a great way to expose a baby to more words in fun and interesting ways and can help parents get into the habit of using lots of different kinds of words, now and for years to come.

THINGS YOU NEED – Yourself, baby, plain yogurt, food colouring, piece of cardboard, printed image

SPECIAL THINGS TO REMEMBER – This will be messy. There is no way to avoid it! Make sure your baby is wearing old clothes, a smock or just a diaper to make cleaning up a little easier.

ACTIVITY – Print out an image from the Internet that your baby might find interesting (e.g., picture of farm animals, cartoon characters, vehicles, etc.), then tape this image to a piece of cardboard to provide some extra stability. Next, mix up some baby-safe "paint" (e.g., one tablespoon of plain yogurt and one drop of food colouring). Three or four different colours are plenty. Place each pot of "paint" on the table so your baby can see them but they are out of their reach. Sit your baby in their highchair and place the image on their tray, then offer them one of the "paint" pots. Show them how to dip their fingers into the "paint" and finger paint on the image. Offer them more "paints" when they seem like they are ready. Continue the activity for as long your baby is interested.

MY BABY WILL – Begin finger painting on the image and explore the materials provided.

THEN I WILL – Use parallel talk as my baby paints. I will also choose one or two new words that go along with the activity or image to repeat often as we do the activity together. For ideas on different types of words to expose your baby to see the list on p.75.

TIP

Babies at this age love to hear words repeated over and over again. If possible, do the same activity, with the same items, a few times during the week so your baby will become familiar with these words and their meanings.

SONGS TO ADD TO YOUR DAILY ROUTINES

Good Morning Song (when greeting them in the morning at their crib)
The good morning train is coming how are you? Choo choo!
The good morning train is coming how are you? Choo choo!
The good morning train is coming, the good morning train is coming, the good morning train is coming how are you? Choo choo!
And we say hello to Timmy, how are you? Choo choo!
And we say hello to Timmy, how are you? Choo choo!
And we say hello to Timmy, and we say hello to Timmy, and we say hello to Timmy, how are you? Choo choo!!

Head and shoulders, knees and toes (while dressing)
Head and shoulders, knees and toes, knees and toes, knees and toes
Head and shoulders, knees and toes,
Eyes, ears, mouth and nose.

If you're happy and you know it wash your… (during bath time)
If you're happy and you know it wash your arm! Scrub, scrub!
If you're happy and you know it wash your arm! Scrub, scrub!
If you're happy and you know it and you really want to show it,
If you're happy and you know it wash your arm! Scrub, scrub!

Rock-a-bye baby (before naps)
Rock-a-bye baby, on the tree top.
When the wind blows, the cradle will rock.
When the bow breaks, the cradle will fall.
But I will catch baby, cradle and all.

ITEMS TO ADD TO THE DISCOVERY DRAWER

Household items:
- plastic cups
- plastic water bottles (lids secured tightly)
- wooden spoons
- plastic bowls or containers
- baby clothes (shirt, pants, socks, etc.)
- cloths with different patterns and textures
- brush
- small shoe
- baby safe mirror
- small empty boxes
- family photographs
- different hats
- measuring cups

Toys:
- teddy bears or dolls
- plastic toy animals
- balls
- blocks
- books
- pretend plastic food
- rattles or shakers
- small musical instruments
- toy vehicles
- small shape sorter
- small insert puzzle

Anything that is safe for your baby to explore with their hands and mouth can go in the drawer!

BABY ART IDEAS

"Paint" with water
Tape a piece of dark coloured construction paper to a place your baby can reach. Allow them to dip a clean paintbrush in water and encourage them to make marks on the paper with the brush.

Stamp it!
Place an empty cardboard box in front of your baby. Give them a plastic animal toy and let them dip the feet into the baby-safe "paint" described previously (p.71). Show your baby how to make stamps by banging the animal's feet onto the cardboard box.

Exploring sensations art
Mix one drop of food colouring into the water in each ice cube tray section and freeze overnight. Place an old towel or sheet down for your baby to sit on. Provide them with one coloured ice cube at a time and let them rub it freely on the material. When they have finished, press a piece of white paper onto the sheet or towel to preserve some of their masterpiece.

DIFFERENT TYPES OF WORDS

Nouns:
These are words generally used for people, places or objects.
Ex: mommy, kitchen or ball

Verbs:
These are words that either express actions or are used to "help" another verb express meaning.
Ex: run or *am* walking

Prepositions:
These are words that typically express spatial or temporal relationships.
Ex: in, on, under, before, after

Pronouns:
Words that can take the place of nouns in a sentence.
Ex: I, you, mine, we, they

Adjectives:
Words that modify nouns by describing a particular quality.
Ex: big, hot, wet, old, shiny

8 MONTHS OLD

WEEK 33: MONKEY SEE, MONKEY DO – AN IMITATION GAME

AREA ADDRESSED –
Pragmatic/Social Language

SKILL TARGETED – Imitates simple one-step actions

WHY DO THIS? – Human beings learn social skills by watching others and imitating what they are doing. Even at this young age babies are watching adult behaviours to learn how to interact with people around them. Providing babies with lots of opportunities to watch and copy simple actions gives them a chance to practice their imitation skills and learn the relationship between their actions and the actions of another person.

> **If You're Happy And You Know It**
>
> If you're happy and you know it clap your hands.
> If you're happy and you know it clap your hands.
> If you're happy and you know it and you really want to show it,
> If you're happy and you know it clap your hands.
>
> If you're happy and you know it kick your feet
> If you're happy and you know it shout hooray (raise arms up and shout hooray)!

THINGS YOU NEED – Yourself and baby

SPECIAL THINGS TO REMEMBER – The more familiar a baby is with a song and its actions, and the more fun they have interacting with an adult while they are singing, the more likely it will be that they will engage with the activity and try and copy the actions.

ACTIVITY – Sit face-to-face with your baby. Start singing the song If You're Happy And You Know It, including doing the simple one-step actions for each verse, modeled clearly for your baby to see. Sing the first verse twice to familiarize your baby with the actions. Then sing the verse a third time, pausing in the song after completing the action to give your baby a chance to copy the behaviour you have just modeled.

MY BABY WILL – Watch me and attempt to copy my actions. They may make babbling noises while we are singing.

THEN I WILL – Smile and praise them for copying what I have done and continue singing the song, adding in more verses. If my baby doesn't copy my actions after singing a few times, I will sing the verse again and gently prompt them to copy me. I will continue practicing the same song every day for the rest of the week until my baby can join in with the actions.

TIP

Choosing the right time in your baby's daily routine will make this activity go more smoothly. Try and find a time in your day when your baby has lots of energy and is ready to play! Since this activity requires no materials, it can really be done anywhere or anytime that works for you and your baby.

WEEK 34: WHAT WILL WE READ TODAY? – BABY'S CHOICE

AREA ADDRESSED – Early Literacy

SKILL TARGETED – Print motivation

WHY DO THIS? – Print motivation is an early literacy skill. It is the thought that books and reading are fun and includes a desire to engage with literacy materials. The kinds of interactions a baby has with their parents surrounding storybook reading affects their growing knowledge and attitudes towards reading, even at this young age. A great way to start to establish print motivation with infants is to read books based on their interests. Offering your baby a choice of what to read can facilitate print motivation and is easy to add into your regular reading routine.

THINGS YOU NEED – Yourself, baby, books

SPECIAL THINGS TO REMEMBER – Books are a great way to help develop an infant's early vocabulary because they offer a natural way to repeat language, provide a wide range of vocabulary, and offer pictures as clues to word meanings. So even if your baby chooses the same book 100 times, they can still learn more from time 101!

ACTIVITY – Place a basket of your baby's favourite books in their room down low where they can access them easily. Before reading, encourage your baby to choose a book they would like to read, either by offering them the whole basket to choose from, or holding up a choice of two books.

MY BABY WILL – Pick a book by pointing, reaching or looking at the one they are interested in.

THEN I WILL – Read the book they have chosen, pointing to pictures and encouraging interactions from my baby during reading. I will re-read the book for as long as my baby is interested.

TIP

Try and rotate the books in the basket every two weeks to offer diverse options.

WEEK 35: "GOING TO GET YOUR….." - A VERBAL ROUTINE

AREA ADDRESSED – Receptive Language

SKILL TARGETED – Learning meaning for familiar words

WHY DO THIS? – Babies need to hear words over and over again before they can learn their meanings and routines offer a natural way of including word repetition into daily life. Routines also have the benefit of teaching babies how their world is organized, the words that are associated with certain activities, each person's role in these activities, and how they can participate. Talking during daily routines is great for a baby's language development but setting up smaller routines in play also offers a simple, yet powerful, opportunity for repeated exposure to some new words and their associated meanings.

THINGS YOU NEED – Yourself and baby

SPECIAL THINGS TO REMEMBER – If you are going to tweak this activity or try and create your own unique verbal routine, think of it like writing a short script - everyone is assigned a role, everyone knows what is expected of them in that role, and the sequence of events is determined beforehand. Also, short and simple is best!

ACTIVITY – Sit your baby down on the sofa and tell them you are going to play a game together. Sit across from them and slowly walk your fingers up their leg to their belly. As you walk your fingers slowly say, "I'm….going to…..get….your…." then pause holding your fingers above their belly. Next bring your fingers down and say, "belly!" as you tickle their belly.

MY BABY WILL – Become more familiar with the game and words each time we play. They will show excitement and anticipation when I pause and may even reach for my hand to pull it down to their belly.

THEN I WILL – Repeat the activity with my baby for as long as they are happy to do so. Once my baby gets familiar with this verbal routine I will try and introduce a new word into the routine (e.g., ears, toes, nose, cheeks, etc.).

TIP

Try adding movement into this activity by encouraging your baby to crawl and try and "escape".

WEEK 36: SCREEN TIME QUIZ – MAKING INFORMED CHOICES IN A DIGITAL AGE

AREA ADDRESSED – Communication Development

SKILL TARGETED – Increasing social interaction with others

WHY DO THIS? – There are many different ways young babies can be exposed to screen time. Understanding how babies learn language, and the effects of screen time on early language development, can help you make more informed choices about how much screen time you decide to expose your baby to now, and in the coming years.

SPECIAL THINGS TO REMEMBER – The Canadian Paediatric Society identifies risks of heavy early screen exposure to significant language delays, attention difficulties, and negative affects to cognitive development and executive functioning for children under five. They recommend no screen time for children under two years of age to ensure a healthy overall development. Please go to their website for more details regarding this topic.

Take the Screen Time Quiz
Answer true or false to the statements below:

1) Having a TV on in the background (e.g., the news) while my baby is playing is not exposing them to screen time if they are not interested in watching the program themselves.
2) The best way for my baby to learn new words is from an application on my phone or tablet.
3) It is important I expose my baby to a small amount of screen time so they can become familiar with its use in this digital age.
4) Using Skype or FaceTime will not aversely affect my baby's language development because they are interacting with another person.
5) Giving my phone to my baby to play with while I am busy is not a big deal and won't affect their language development because it is only for a small amount of time.
6) Screen time in early childhood has been linked to language delays, cognitive delays, obesity and behaviour problems at school age.
7) I want my baby to learn another language and giving them a chance to learn these new words from an app is the best way to do it.
8) Screen time is an issue in early development because it takes young children away from activities that are known to benefit their overall development.
9) My baby is looking at the screen, smiling and laughing with pleasure so they must be learning something.
10) I know people who let their young children watch TV and use iPhone and iPad apps all the time and their children talk a lot. As long as my child is talking there should be no need to worry about screen time use.

Answers: 1) F 2) F 3) F 4) T (maybe) 5) F 6) T 7) F 8) T 9) F 10) F

GREAT ACTION SONGS FOR BABIES AND TODDLERS

The Grand Old Duke of York
The Grand old Duke of York, he had 10,000 men.
He marched them up and down the hill (arms up and down),
And he marched them up again.
And when they're up, they're up (arms up),
And when they're down, they're down (arms down),
And when they're only halfway up they're neither up nor down.
So march them to the left (move arms to the side),
And march them to the right (move arms to the other side),
March them up and down again (arms up and down),
And march the out of sight (bring hands into your lap).

The Itsy Bitsy Spider
The Itsy Bitsy spider went up the water spout (wiggle fingers while raising hands upwards).
Down came the rain and washed the spider out (bring hands down slowly).
Out came the sun and dried up all the rain (raise arms up).
So the Itsy Bitsy spider went up the spout again (wiggle fingers while raising hands upwards).

Roly Poly
Roly poly, roly poly,
Up, up, up. Up, up, up (lift arms up).
Roly, roly, poly, roly, roly poly,
Down, down, down. Down, down, down (bring arms down).

Roly, poly, roly poly,
Clap, clap, clap. Clap, clap, clap (clapping hands),
Roly, roly, poly, roly, roly, poly,
Kick, kick, kick. Kick, kick, kick (kick feet).

VERBAL ROUTINES TO TRY

Ring-Around-The-Rosie
Tell your baby you are going to do a dance together. Pick them up and start to sing Ring-Around-The-Rosie, walking slowly around in a circle with your baby as you sing. When you start to sing the final words (e.g., all fall down), "tumble" to the floor with your baby. Stress the word *down* as you come down to the floor to help your baby learn the meaning for this word.

Airplane In The Sky
Pick your baby up and tell them they are going to go on a special airplane ride today. Start to make engine noises (e.g., "vroom vroom"). Next say "Let's go!", then gently soar your baby around the room as if they were flying, making airplane noises as you do (e.g., "zoom zoom"). Try and stress the word *go* to help your baby become familiar with the meaning for this word. After a few minutes tell them "It is time to come for a landing" and gently place them down on the sofa.

Pour And Dump At Bath Time
Place two plastic cups into the bathtub during your baby's bath time. Pick up the cups. Fill one with water and ensure the other is empty. Then say, "Pour….pour….. pour". Each time you say the word "pour", pour some of the water from the cup that is full into the cup that is empty. Then hold the newly filled cup in front of your baby and say "Dump!" as you dump all the water from this cup back into the bathtub. Allow your baby to participate in this routine to the best of their abilities.

Verbal routines should be repeated regularly so your baby can become familiar with the words and their meanings for that particular routine.

9 MONTHS OLD

WEEK 37: PUPPET JARGON

AREA ADDRESSED – Expressive Language

SKILL TARGETED – Uses a wide variety of speech sounds

WHY DO THIS? – Vocal development is the process babies go through as they learn to produce and control the speech sounds in their language(s). Two important things play a key role in how well and how fast babies will move through the stages of vocal development as they progress toward saying first words; the experience they have hearing lots of speech sounds from adults in their lives, and the experience they have hearing their own voice as they make different speech sounds. Activities that encourage back-and-forth "conversations" with babies, even before they can talk, are such a powerful way to support vocal development and encourage first words and beyond, because they allow babies the opportunity to have both kinds of experiences in one activity.

THINGS YOU NEED – Yourself, baby, puppet

SPECIAL THINGS TO REMEMBER – Your baby is entering the final stage of vocal development before they will say their first word. Over the next few months they will begin to combine different consonants and vowels together, which is known as non-reduplicated babbling. They may also include prosody (e.g., the melodic tone of language) while they babble, almost making it sound like they are actually talking to you.

ACTIVITY – Find an old white sock and draw a face at the toe end. If you have time get creative and use other items from around the house to make your puppet look interesting and fun to talk to! Sit face-to-face with your baby and put the puppet on your hand. Introduce the puppet to your baby by giving it a funny name and a funny voice, then start having the puppet talk to your baby.

MY BABY WILL – Engage with the puppet by reaching out to touch it. They may make different speech sounds as they play and explore.

THEN I WILL – Encourage my baby to play and interact with the puppet by having the puppet do silly things or actions my baby might find interesting and fun. As we play, I will try and establish a back-and-forth "conversation" between my baby and the puppet (e.g., baby babbles - puppet talks – baby babbles – puppet talks).

TIP

Keep the puppet by the change table so your baby can have daily chats with their new friend each day!

WEEK 38: THE FAMILY FORT

AREA ADDRESSED – Receptive Language

SKILL TARGETED – Vocabulary development

WHY DO THIS? – The types of activities a parent exposes a child to in their daily life can have a major effect on how much and what kinds of words they are hearing, which in turn has a direct impact on how fast and how well they learn language. Even providing one new language-rich activity into your typical routine, for example with the addition of playing a weekly game together, can have a powerfully positive effect on a child's overall vocabulary growth.

THINGS YOU NEED – Yourself, baby, sofa, blankets, pillows

SPECIAL THINGS TO REMEMBER – This activity is fantastic for bringing out lots of action words (e.g., crawl, peek, hide) and location words (e.g., under, in, on). It is referred to as a guided learning activity, which means the environment has been created to attract the child's attention but includes challenges your baby will require help with to accomplish, for example learning to go under something as you play.

ACTIVITY – Use pillows, blankets and the sofa to build a small fort for you and your baby to crawl in, around, over or under. This is an open-ended activity so there are no rules and no specific beginning or end to the game. Follow your baby's lead as you play and get creative! Use parallel talk, self-talk and gestures while you play with your baby to expose them to new words and their meanings. For ideas on the types of words to include in this activity see p.75.

MY BABY WILL – Explore the fort, going under, over or around the objects. They may make noises or eye contact with me as a sign they are excited to explore and play together. They may also want to bring other items into the fort to make the activity more interesting for them.

THEN I WILL – Get down on the floor and explore the fort with my baby. I will emphasize new words for my baby each time we play, however I will also remember not to do all the talking so my baby can have a chance to add their voice into the game too.

TIP

Try and set up the fort at least once a week so your baby can hear these words often as part of their regular routine.

WEEK 39: PETER POINTER BEDTIME ROUTINE

AREA ADDRESSED – Communication Development

SKILL TARGETED – Engages in joint attention

WHY DO THIS? – Joint attention is when a child and adult both focus on an object or event at the same time. Joint attention is a critical skill infants and toddlers must develop to ensure strong communication skills and language development. Your baby is now at an age where you can direct their attention to an object by pointing; establishing joint attention for that object. Directing a baby's attention through pointing has the benefit of making word meanings more clear for them and also provides a model for your baby of how they can direct your attention to something.

THINGS YOU NEED – Yourself, baby, items around the room

SPECIAL THINGS TO REMEMBER – Don't make this activity last too long. At bedtime babies are tired and will have a very short attention span and patience level. Just pointing to a few things is all that is needed. The most important part is that this powerful language boosting activity becomes part of the daily routine.

ACTIVITY – Just before you put your baby to bed tell them you are going to say goodnight to different things in their room. Hold your baby and walk around the room, then using your extended index finger, point to a few different things that are all ready to "go to sleep". As you point, direct your child's attention to that item (e.g., "Look. There is your teddy. Goodnight teddy.").

MY BABY WILL – Look in the direction I am pointing. They may make noises or sounds or may even try and imitate my pointing.

THEN I WILL – Continue to say goodnight to a few items in the room before putting my baby to bed, trying to encourage my baby to look where I am pointing as we say goodnight to each one.

TIP

If your baby is really fussy before bedtime try adapting this to fit with your morning routine.

WEEK 40: BOOKS O' PLENTY

AREA ADDRESSED – Early Literacy

SKILL TARGETED – Engages with reading materials

WHY DO THIS? – Having access to books is one of the biggest predictors of later literacy success. For babies, the term *access* means that they are able to independently get to books during their regular routines. Having reading materials more easily accessible will increase the opportunity your baby has to explore books on their own and for you to engage with them in more book reading throughout the day.

> **Try Adding Books…**
>
> - near your baby's seat in the car
> - in the stroller
> - in the diaper bag
> - near your baby's highchair
> - in baskets with their toys
> - by the bathtub
> - by the change table
> - by the front door
> - soft books by their crib
> - in a low drawer they can access at home

THINGS YOU NEED – Yourself and books

SPECIAL THINGS TO REMEMBER – Choose books that your baby loves but aren't too precious if they get lost or damaged when taken outside the house. If possible, have multiple copies of your child's favourites so you can keep one in their room and others in different areas.

ACTIVITY – This week you are going to add books to key areas where your baby can access them easily in their daily routine. The aim is to try and find three new locations to keep books accessible for your baby. Place 3-6 books in a few of the locations suggested above, or come up with your own ideas that fit well with your unique family environment.

MY BABY WILL – Engage with these books during the week by exploring, looking or playing with the book.

THEN I WILL – Encourage my baby to access these books during our daily routine. I will give my baby opportunities to explore these books independently, as well as watch for moments to join in with them and look at the book together.

TIP

Set a reminder on the calendar to rotate the books every month to ensure your baby is always offered new and exciting reading material.

FUN GAMES TO PLAY WITH YOUR BABY

Hide and Seek
Take turns hiding around the house or outside and finding each other. Stuffed animals can also have a turn "hiding" and you and your baby can seek them together.

Baby Obstacle Course
Use items from around the house to create an obstacle course for your baby to go over, under and through. Model how the course works for your baby then let them have a turn.

Baby Basketball
Set up a large empty bin in a room. Collect small, light items from around the house and take turns tossing them in the bin with your baby.

Dance Party
Turn on the radio or your favourite song. Pick your baby up and dance around the room singing to the music as you go.

Pillow Slide
Take one of the larger cushions off your sofa and set it up against the side to make a "slide". Help your baby climb up onto the sofa and slide down.

All games should include self-talk, parallel talk and gestures to make them a truly language-rich experience. Also, don't forget to take pauses and wait to give your baby a chance to add their own voice into the game too!

NEW EXPERIENCES FOR YOUR BABY

Ideas for outings you could go on with your baby to expose them to new words:
- the swimming pool
- the park
- a community group
- a library drop-in group
- a museum
- the zoo
- a farm
- a walk in the forest
- a visit to friends and family
- the beach
- the aquarium
- a walk through a new neighbourhood

TIPS FOR READING TO BUSY BABIES

- Choose books based on your baby's interests even if that means reading the same book over and over again.

- Use your voice to make funny sounds and noises that go along with the story to keep your baby's attention.

- Make books interactive by allowing your baby to explore the book their way.

- There are no rules for reading at this age so allow your baby to start and stop the book where they want, as well as go back in pages.

- Encourage movement and actions while reading to make storytime more fun.

- Keep reading time short and simple since babies have very limited attention spans. It is better to read more often for shorter periods, than once for a longer time period.

- Let your child help choose the reading time. Watch for when they have picked up a book and then join in.

9 MONTH MILESTONES AND MEMORIES

Your baby is only a few months away from their first birthday and that much closer to saying their first word! You and your baby have come so far together in this journey. With your help, here is what your baby has learned to do:

	Understanding Language	**Using Language**
6 to 9 Months	Enjoys games such as peek-a-boo and pat-a-cake	Makes a variety of babbling noises
	Appears to listen when spoken to	Imitates simple actions with objects (e.g., bang a drum)
	Recognizes familiar words (e.g., book, cup, mommy)	Uses vocalizations (crying and non-crying) to get an adult's attention
	Begins to respond to simple words and phrases (e.g., "no", "come here", etc.)	Attempts to imitate simple actions (e.g., waving)
	Responds to their own name	Begins to use gestures during interactions with an adult

Here are all the things you are now doing each day to help them prepare to say words:

Singing songs to help my baby recognize familiar words	Using parallel talk while my baby plays	Imitating my baby's sounds and actions
Using art activities to explore more words together	Encouraging my baby to imitate simple actions	Offering a choice in book reading to encourage my baby's interests
Creating verbal routines to learn new word meanings	Making informed choices about screen time for my infant	Using puppets to encourage lots of sounds and noises from my baby
Playing games to teach new word meanings	Modeling pointing during daily interactions to encourage joint attention	Offering easy and abundant access to books throughout the day

9 MONTH MILESTONES AND MEMORIES

PUT A PICTURE OF YOUR BABY HERE

What speech sounds have you heard your baby babbling with (w, y, m, n, p, b, d, t, k, g)?
_____
_____
_____
_____
_____

What kinds of books does your baby like to have you read?
_____
_____
_____
_____
_____

Record a funny memory you had with your baby from these past few months together.
_____
_____
_____
_____
_____

GETTING READY TO SAY FIRST WORDS

10 MONTHS OLD

WEEK 41: MY LITTLE HELPER

AREA ADDRESSED – Receptive Language

SKILL TARGETED – Vocabulary development

WHY DO THIS? – Research shows that 10-month old babies are actively trying to figure out meanings for the new words they hear. They do this by making a few assumptions as they interact in their environment each day. For example, they assume that new words they hear are associated with the most interesting thing they are seeing or doing at the time. A great way to make daily living routines more interesting for a baby is to include them as active participants. Giving your baby a chance to complete actions themselves, or handle objects being talked about, is more engaging for them than being a passive observer and can improve their chances of connecting the correct meaning to the words they hear.

THINGS YOU NEED – Yourself, baby, clothing

SPECIAL THINGS TO REMEMBER – As your baby becomes familiar with the routine, gradually hold back from guiding them to complete the actions. With experience they will learn to follow the directions without your help.

ACTIVITY – Have your baby help you when getting ready for bed. Follow these steps:
 1) Sit together beside the drawer where you keep your baby's pajamas and say, "Let's open the drawer". Pause and guide your baby's hand to the drawer and help them tug it open. While you open the drawer together say, "Open. Let's open the drawer".
 2) Next say, "Let's take out your pajamas". Pause and guide your baby's hand to take out the pajamas. While you take them out say, "Out. Out come the pajamas".
 3) Next say, "It's time to close the drawer". Pause and guide your baby's hand to close the drawer. While you close the drawer say, "Close. Let's close the drawer".

MY BABY WILL – Watch and listen to me and complete the actions with my help.

THEN I WILL – Smile and encourage my baby with facial expressions and words when they have completed the action. This will encourage my little helper to continue engaging with me in this routine and keep it fun.

TIP

Use the word list on p.102 to inspire you to find other ways your little helper can become involved in daily routines.

WEEK 42: FOLLOW THE LEADER – WATCHING A BABY'S NON-VERBAL COMMUNICATION

AREA ADDRESSED – Expressive Language

SKILL TARGETED – Uses gestures to communicate

WHY DO THIS? – Gestures and language are tightly coupled neurologically and developmentally. When infants are between 9-13 months old they begin to establish a repertoire of gestures to communicate messages to adults. The more an adult can tune-in to this form of early communication and respond appropriately to a baby's messages, the better it is for their language development. In fact, studies show caregivers who are more responsive to these early communication attempts tend to have babies who talk sooner and reach the 50 word milestone at a younger age.

THINGS YOU NEED – Yourself and baby

SPECIAL THINGS TO REMEMBER – Remember, your baby is the leader on this outing. Allow them to lead the interactions by exploring what they are interested in, talking about what they are looking at or gesturing to, and establishing a back-and-forth "conversation" as you interact.

ACTIVITY – Go on an outing together somewhere your baby would enjoy. This could be the park, a museum, a farm visit or another place that will be new and exciting for your baby (see ideas for outings on p.91). During the outing make a point of observing how your baby communicates without words. Use the example sheet on p.103 for the kinds of things to look for and record any other ways your baby is using gestures to communicate with you.

MY BABY WILL – Engage with the items and activities in the environment. They will use eye contact, facial expressions and gestures to send messages to me while we interact on the outing.

THEN I WILL – Observe my baby's attempts at communication. After they use a gesture to communicate with me I will interpret their message, then make a comment and respond appropriately.

TIP

Letting your baby be the leader will involve a lot of waiting and might feel uncomfortable at first. However, this won't always be the case as your baby gets more practice using gestures to communicate and you get better at interpreting their messages.

WEEK 43: TOWER, TALK AND TUMBLE

AREA ADDRESSED – Receptive Language

SKILL TARGETED – Vocabulary development

WHY DO THIS? – At this age babies enjoy hearing words repeated over and over again. Research shows that when caregivers incorporate repetition of words during interactions with their babies, these children go on to have larger vocabularies. Simple play routines are perfect for exposing babies to word repetition. That's because at this stage a baby's play is mainly about discovering cause and effect, so they enjoy toys and play activities that allow them to repeat the same actions over and over again.

THINGS YOU NEED – Yourself, baby, blocks or plastic cups of different sizes

SPECIAL THINGS TO REMEMBER – It may seem silly to play with your baby and repeat a word over and over again, however keep in mind that this is exactly how your baby wants to play at this age. Choose one word that would naturally occur during any activity and repeat it for your baby as you play.

ACTIVITY – Sit across from your baby with the blocks between you. Tell them you are going to build a tower. Start to build the tower one block at a time and talk to your baby about what you are doing (e.g., "This will be a big tower! Let's get the blocks."). Each time you or your baby stack a block use the word *on* as the block is being stacked (e.g., "This block goes *on*. Now this block is *on*."). When all the blocks are stacked say, "One, two, three…down they go!" and knock the blocks over with your baby. Repeat the activity for as long as your baby is interested to play.

MY BABY WILL – Watch and listen or try and stack blocks with my help.

THEN I WILL – Talk to my baby about what we are doing, repeating the word *on* each time we stack a block. I will also try and take turns with my baby during this activity (e.g., baby stacks a block, then I stack a block). After we have completed the tower I will encourage my baby to knock it over.

TIP

Use the list provided on p.104 to find other play activities that have naturally occurring repetition patterns to add more word repetition into playtime with your baby.

WEEK 44: CHOICE OF TWO, WHAT WILL YOU DO?

AREA ADDRESSED – Expressive Language

SKILL TARGETED – Uses gestures to communicate

WHY DO THIS? – Pointing is a key milestone in language development that emerges between 7–15 months of age and develops over a baby's second year of life. Early pointing abilities in infants have been linked to larger vocabularies and expressive language skills as toddlers. Finding regular ways to offer opportunities for your baby to practice pointing to communicate is beneficial to their overall language development and easy to add into many typical daily routines.

THINGS YOU NEED – Yourself, baby, food items

SPECIAL THINGS TO REMEMBER – Firstly, when your baby makes a choice you want to be able to give them what they have asked for so make sure both options offered are parent approved. Secondly, make sure your baby actually wants at least one of the items you're holding. They need to be motivated to make a choice for this activity to work effectively.

ACTIVITY – Sit your baby in their highchair ready to eat. Have two desired food options available on the table in your baby's view but out of their reach. Sit across from your baby then ask them what they want to eat, pointing to each item as you offer that choice. For example say, "Do you want apple sauce (while pointing to the apple sauce) or do you want a muffin (while pointing to the muffin)?" Next, be patient and wait, giving your baby a chance to make a choice.

MY BABY WILL – Watch and listen, then try and reach or point to the item they want.

THEN I WILL – Pass them the item they have pointed to/reached for while labeling the item (e.g., "Here is your apple sauce!"). If I have asked my baby the question three times and they still have not made a choice, I will hold the items in each hand and bring them directly in front of my baby. I will repeat the question and watch for a sign for which item they might prefer, either with a gesture or by looking at one particular item, then offer that item.

TIP

Make sure you have your baby's attention and that they are looking at each item while you offer the choices.

WORDS TYPCIALLY FOUND IN EARLY VOCABULARIES

Verbs	Nouns
kiss	dog
eat	ball
drink	book
hug	cup
dance	juice
wipe	shoes
wash	banana
give	keys
climb	cookie
tickle	bathtub
open	bed
blow	spoon
jump	teddy bear
throw	socks
play	door
get	brush
look	apple
bring	chair
splash	hat
push	shirt
slide	stairs
hold	window
close	finger
clap	nose
kick	mouth
pull	doll
pour	hand

EXAMPLES OF EARLY NON-VERBAL COMMUNICATION

Reasons Your Baby Might Communicate	Example	Gestures You Might See Your Baby Use	What You Might Say In Response	Additional Comments To Add Next
Answer a question	Parent asks, "Do you see the dog?"	Point, reach	"Yes! The dog!"	"Dogs say woof woof."
Call attention to something	Baby sees a shovel in the sandbox	Point or pick up object and show	"A shovel."	"Let's dig with the shovel."
Greetings	Grandma comes to the park and says, "Hi" to baby	Wave	"Hi Grandma"	"Let's ask Grandma to play."
Protests	You offer baby a ball to play with	Turns head, throws object down	"No. Ok no ball right now."	"Look. We can try the slide."
Make requests	You bring baby to the swings	Reach arms up, point to the swing	"The swing. Ok let's put you in the swing."	"Ready for a big push!"

Other ways I have observed my baby communicate with gestures:
_____
_____
_____
_____
_____

PLAYING WITH YOUR BABY

Activities that involve repetition:
- pop-up toys
- putting a ball in a net or basket
- driving a car down a ramp
- blowing bubbles
- banging a drum or piano
- putting pieces in insert puzzles
- stacking nesting cups
- going down a slide
- pushing on a swing
- moving beads along a Busy Bead toy
- peek-a-boo
- pushing buttons on a noisy book

FIVE WAYS TO ADD CHOICES INTO YOUR DAILY ROUTINE

1) Getting ready to go out
    Ex: "Should we put on your shoes or your hat?"

2) Nap time
    Ex: "Do you want to sleep with a teddy or doll?"

3) Bath time
    Ex: "Would you like to play with the boat or the duck?"

4) Getting dressed
    Ex: "Should we start with your shirt or socks?"

5) Play
    Ex: "Do you want to play with a ball or a car?"

Don't forget to hold each item up so your baby can gesture to make a choice!

11 MONTHS OLD

WEEK 45: RULE OF THUMB IS 5:1

AREA ADDRESSED – Receptive Language

SKILL TARGETED – Identifies common objects in books

WHY DO THIS? – At this age your baby should have several words in their vocabulary even though they may not be saying anything yet. Asking your baby to identify different pictures in a book lets you see what vocabulary they have already learned, and is a great way for you to show them new word meanings to enrich their growing language skills. Studies show that babies with larger vocabularies go on to have better language and reading skills at kindergarten and shared book reading is known to be one of the best ways to develop vocabulary in young children.

THINGS YOU NEED – Yourself, baby, book

SPECIAL THINGS TO REMEMBER – Nobody likes being tested and babies are no exception. The Rule of Thumb is 5:1 is a guideline for reading with young children that encourages adults to make five statements for every one question asked. When you keep this idea in mind it will help ensure book reading remains fun for your baby instead of a quiz while still encouraging a little language learning too. If your baby is keen, let them show you other items in the book while you are following the Rule of Thumb is 5:1 guideline.

ACTIVITY – Sit with your baby in a comfortable position where you are face-to-face. Begin looking at the book together and point out different things you see in the pictures (e.g., "Look, there is a cow. I see the pig. There are the chickens."). After five statements about what you see in the book ask your baby to show you an item on the page (e.g., "Can you show me the horse?"). After your baby responds continue the Rule of Thumb is 5:1 method as you look through the rest of the book together.

MY BABY WILL – a) Point to the correct picture of the item you have asked.
b) Point to the incorrect picture or make no response.

THEN I WILL – a) Say, "Yes! That is the horse!"
b) Show my baby the correct image by pointing and saying, "There is the horse!" Then encourage my baby to show me the horse again (e.g., "Let's see if you can find that horse again! Can you show me where that horse is?"). If they then point to the correct picture I will tell them they are right. If they make an error again or make no response, I will show them the correct picture then continue on with the book.

TIP

Use books that have pictures of common or familiar items your baby may interact with each day. Although almost any book will do, you can also use the recommended book list on p.62 for great book ideas for this activity.

WEEK 46: SILLY SOUNDS WITH PLAY DOUGH

AREA ADDRESSED – Expressive Language

SKILL TARGETED – Imitates sounds in play

WHY DO THIS? – Encouraging your baby to imitate what you say is very important at this age. That's because imitating small sounds helps babies practice for the more complicated task of imitating words. Studies show that babies who are better at imitating sounds generally go on to have more advanced language skills as toddlers.

THINGS YOU NEED – Yourself, baby, taste-safe play dough, small toys

SPECIAL THINGS TO REMEMBER – At this age your baby is still getting the hang of making speech sounds. It is normal for babies to try and imitate the sounds and words they are hearing but not to have it come out exactly the same (e.g., "wah" for water or "ta" for car). The most important thing at this age is that they are trying to imitate what they hear to the best of their abilities.

ACTIVITY – Place your baby in their highchair then seat yourself across from them so you are facing one another. Place a small amount of taste-safe play dough (recipe on p.112) on your baby's tray. Show them how to manipulate it with their hands then let them explore. As you play together, make some silly sounds that go along with what you are doing (e.g., say "boof" as you pat the play dough down, or say "puh, puh" as you squish it together). Include some small toys in this activity as well and make the noises associated with these items as you play (e.g., say "toot toot" when playing with a train or say "quack quack" when playing with a duck).

MY BABY WILL – Play with the taste-safe play dough and try and imitate my sounds and/or use their own sounds as we play together.

THEN I WILL – Repeat the sound for a specific item or action over and over again as we play. I will allow lots of pauses to occur while I talk, giving my baby a chance to try and imitate what I have said. When I think my baby has tried to imitate my sounds I will smile, praise them, then repeat the sound again. I will continue playing with my baby for as long as they are interested in the activity.

TIP

Although this play dough is made with natural ingredients it is not meant to be eaten. If your baby is still putting many things in their mouth while they play, modify this activity and use water instead.

WEEK 47: A LITTLE BIT OF SABOTAGE GOES A LONG WAY

AREA ADDRESSED – Expressive Language

SKILL TARGETED – Uses gestures to communicate

WHY DO THIS? – Early "conversations" between an adult and baby are an essential part of a healthy language development. Research shows that these types of back-and-forth exchanges are just as important to language learning as how many words a young child hears. Interactions that encourage the use of gestures and sounds to communicate should be incorporated as often as possible into typical daily living to help ensure a child develops strong language abilities.

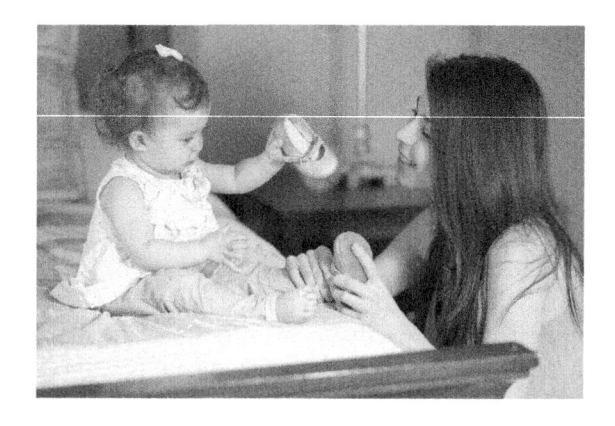

THINGS YOU NEED – Yourself, baby, shoes

SPECIAL THINGS TO REMEMBER – Life with young children tends to be very busy and often it is faster and easier to do things for your baby throughout the day. However, this is not the best approach for supporting a baby's growing language skills. Giving your baby a chance to use their developing communication skills during daily routines to request the things they need, reject the things they don't want, or show you the things that interest them, will help them learn the power of communication and also encourage them to use words when they are ready.

ACTIVITY – Just before you are ready to leave the house place your baby's shoes nearby in a location where they can be seen by your baby but they are out of reach. As you get ready to leave, show them you are putting your own shoes on. Then wait expectantly next to your baby's shoes, allowing them the opportunity to request to have their own shoes be put on too.

MY BABY WILL – Use a gesture to communicate with me, for example point to or reach for their shoes. They may also use sounds or words to go along with their gesture.

THEN I WILL – Say, "Shoes! You need shoes!" and put the shoes on for your baby. If my baby does not make an attempt to communicate with me I will try and prompt them to make a response by saying things like, "Oh no! You can't go without shoes!" or draw their attention to the shoes by pointing or saying, "Look, there are your shoes!"

TIP

Avoid asking your baby to use words (e.g., "Can you ask mommy for your shoes?"). Sabotage is about setting the stage and going with the flow. The keys to success are practice and finding the balance between encouragement and frustration.

WEEK 48: PEEK-A-BOO HI AND BYE

AREA ADDRESSED – Expressive Language

SKILL TARGETED – Uses gestures to communicate

WHY DO THIS? – Having lots of different reasons to communicate is important for a baby's growing language skills. Asking for things, showing things and rejecting things are important functions of communication that help a baby learn to navigate their interactions with others. However, babies also need to learn the social part of communication, including sharing greetings with others as they come and go.

THINGS YOU NEED – Yourself, baby, a blanket

SPECIAL THINGS TO REMEMBER – Make your waving gesture very clear and ensure it lasts for several seconds so your baby has a good opportunity to see what they are expected to imitate.

ACTIVITY – Sit across from your baby and tell them you are going to play Peek-a-Boo. Wave bye-bye to your baby and encourage them to wave bye-bye to you too. Then put the blanket over your head and be quiet for a few seconds. Next say, "Where did I go? Where is mommy/daddy?" Allow the blanket to come off, either by you taking it off or your baby pulling it off, then look happy and excited to see your baby. Say, "Hi!" while waving, maybe adding in a few kisses and cuddles afterwards. Repeat the activity until your baby signals they have tired of the game.

MY BABY WILL – Imitate waving at appropriate times in the game. They may use sounds, or even try to imitate my words while we are playing.

THEN I WILL – Use facial expressions, words and actions that my baby enjoys to keep them having fun and engaged with the game. I will praise them when they imitate my actions, sounds or words as we play the game together. If my baby does not imitate my waving gesture, I will gently try and prompt them to do so at appropriate times in the game.

TIP

Try and find more ways to practice by modifying this game to include your baby's favourite stuffed toys and remembering to incorporate natural greetings throughout the day as you see different people.

TASTE-SAFE PLAY DOUGH RECIPE

Ingredients:
- 1 cup cornstarch or corn flour
- 1½ cups of baby rice cereal
- 3 tbsp vegetable oil
- ¼ cup fruit puree of your choice
- 1 tbsp water

Directions:
1) Pour the dry ingredients into a large bowl.
2) Add the vegetable oil and fruit puree, combining well with an electric mixer.
3) If the mixture is too sticky, add more baby rice cereal until you have the desired consistency. It should be pliable and be able to hold its shape without crumbling. If the mixture is too dry add more water until the desired consistency is reached.
4) Remove from the bowl and knead by hand until smooth.

Store this taste-safe play dough in a sealed container in the fridge. Discard after two days. Please keep in mind that this is not intended to be food and parents should discourage consumption. If you suspect your baby has any allergies or sensitivities to the ingredients listed above, modify this activity and use water instead. Safety should always be the first priority!

IDEAS FOR LANGUAGE LEARNING SABOTAGE DURING DAILY ROUTINES

Requesting Things:
- At mealtime place a desired food item in your baby's view but slightly out of their reach, and WAIT.
- At bath time hold toys in your hand instead of putting them into the tub right away, and WAIT.
- When coming to get your baby after they have been sleeping, stand by the crib, and WAIT.
- When playing games together pause just before their favourite part in the activity, and WAIT.
- Stand near the toy box with your baby but don't open it immediately, then WAIT.

Rejecting Things:
- At mealtime offer your baby their least preferred food item, and WAIT.
- Offer your baby their least preferred toy during playtime, then WAIT.
- When going out, offer your baby the wrong shoe to wear, then WAIT.

Showing Things:
- When something falls from your baby's highchair don't pick it up right away, WAIT.
- On an outing, if you both observe something interesting don't make a comment right away, WAIT.
- Be silly by doing unexpected things, like putting your baby's shoes on your head, then WAIT.
- Open a book to a page you think your baby might be interested in, and WAIT.
- Give your baby a toy to play with that they might find interesting, then WAIT.

12 MONTHS OLD

WEEK 49: FILL IT IN BABY!

AREA ADDRESSED – Expressive Language

SKILL TARGETED – Uses sounds or words in familiar songs

WHY DO THIS? – By this age your baby has developed all the skills needed to make words. From this point forward learning how to talk is mainly about practice and experience so it's important you give your baby lots of opportunities to use their voice. One easy way to do this is by allowing them the chance to fill in sounds or words during songs they are familiar with. Singing is a perfect way to encourage babies to use their voices since they have heard the words in the songs often, therefore they will have an idea of what they are expected to say or do, and the activity is highly motivating.

THINGS YOU NEED – Yourself and baby

SPECIAL THINGS TO REMEMBER – Don't be discouraged if your baby does not use sounds or words during the song right away. It may take some practice before they realize you have changed the routine and now want them to start adding in their own voice along with yours. Just keep practicing and soon you will be singing along together.

ACTIVITY – Over the past year you have been singing lots of songs to your baby and they probably have some favourites. Choose their most preferred song for this activity, then pick your baby up, come face-to-face, and start to sing. Being face-to-face is very important in this activity as it encourages more sound and word use from babies. When you get to your baby's favourite part in the song, pause and give them a chance to fill in that portion with a sound or even a word.

MY BABY WILL – Become excited when I am about to sing their favourite part of a familiar song. When I pause, my baby will make a sound or attempt to fill in the word to go along with that portion of the song.

THEN I WILL – Smile and encourage my baby for trying to talk! I will continue singing the rest of the song, allowing other pauses to occur while I sing so my baby can have additional opportunities to fill in parts of the song with more sounds or words.

TIP

Stick with the same song, pausing at the same point, until your baby can fill in the pause with a sound or word before moving on to pausing at other parts or trying this activity with a new song.

WEEK 50: OUR DAILY TALKING GAME

AREA ADDRESSED – Expressive Language

SKILL TARGETED – Uses sounds or words to communicate

WHY DO THIS? – Research shows that when babies say their first words, these are generally words that are said in a highly familiar, routinely occurring situation. Setting up a daily talking game based on your baby's unique interests, for five minutes each day, that happens at the same time and in the same place, can help prepare them to say words from that particular routine and much more!

THINGS YOU NEED – Yourself, baby, a balloon

SPECIAL THINGS TO REMEMBER – If your facial expression remains happy and excited as you interact with your baby, they will likely want to play this game with you longer. To encourage word use ensure you are face-to-face as you play and include lots of waiting as a cue to your baby that they are expected to do or say something.

ACTIVITY – Tell your baby you are going to play with a balloon and it will do some silly tricks. Show them the balloon then begin to blow it up slowly, saying "blow" in an excited tone each time you blow air in. Once the balloon is blown up say, "Ok. Are you ready for the balloon to be silly?" then raise the balloon over your head and release the end allowing it to fly around the room. When the balloon lands on the floor show your baby where it has landed and go to it together. Allow your baby the chance to pick up the balloon and communicate with you about what they would like to happen next.

MY BABY WILL – Pick up the balloon, reach over and give it to me to blow up again. They will also use a sound or a word, along with the gesture, to make this request.

THEN I WILL – Say, "The balloon! Ok, let's blow it up again!" and repeat the activity again. If my baby does not make a sound, I will prompt them to do so by saying "balloon", then waiting for them to try and imitate me. If they then attempt a sound or word I will smile and encourage them for trying to talk, then blow up the balloon. If my baby does not use a sound or word after prompting them three times I will simply move on and continue with the game.

TIP

Find more daily talking games on p.120 for other ways to encourage your baby to talk or try your own unique ideas!

WEEK 51: WORD TOSS – TEACHING CATEGORIES FOR WORD LEARNING

AREA ADDRESSED – Receptive Language

SKILL TARGETED – Categorization of words

WHY DO THIS? – To become efficient word learners babies must be able to link words together that have certain properties in common. This is known as categorization. Even before they can talk babies' brains start organizing the words they have learned into specific categories. They then use these categories to help them learn accurate meanings for each new word they hear. Studies show that babies who are more precise at categorizing nouns have stronger language skills as toddlers.

THINGS YOU NEED – Yourself, baby, household objects or toys

SPECIAL THINGS TO REMEMBER – Keeping this game fun by making silly sounds, adding lots of movement or including other family members, will ensure your baby stays engaged with this activity for longer periods.

ACTIVITY – Choose two categories from the list provided on p.121. Next, gather ten household items or toys (five from each category) and put them inside two buckets. Sit in front of your baby and let them watch you dump both buckets upside down, allowing the items to scatter on the floor. Say to your baby, "Oh no! I made a mess. I'm so silly. Can you help me put everything back where it belongs? I'll go first." Then pick up an item and toss it into a specific category bucket. Label the item you have picked up and tell your baby what category/bucket this item belongs to (e.g., "Here is a cow. He needs to go back in the animal bucket." or "Here is a shirt. It needs to go back in the clothes bucket."). Toss each item into the correct bucket until they have all been picked up.

MY BABY WILL – Watch me and try to participate by picking up items and putting them into the buckets. They may try and use sounds or words as we communicate during the activity together.

THEN I WILL – Put a few items into their correct buckets, then encourage my baby to put the remaining items away by asking where certain things belong (e.g., "Where does the horse go?"). As we play, I will support my baby as they put all items into the correct category buckets one at a time.

TIP

This game can be easily incorporated into your tidy up routine at the end of the day.

WEEK 52: LET'S PRETEND – READY, SET, COPY ME!

AREA ADDRESSED – Receptive Language and Play Development

SKILL TARGETED – Imitates one-step actions in pretend play

WHY DO THIS? – Play and language development are strongly related. Research shows that when a baby engages in simple one-step pretend play actions, this behaviour promotes language and cognitive development. Studies also show that when parents engage in pretend play activities with their toddlers, in a supportive and positive way, these children increase the amount of pretend play they do and engage in more advanced play at earlier ages.

THINGS YOU NEED – Yourself, baby, teddy, spoon, bowl

SPECIAL THINGS TO REMEMBER – As your baby grows over this next year they will start to add other simple pretend activities into their play; at first starting with simple one-step actions, then combining two or three-step action sequences. It is important you continue to encourage these simple pretend sequences over the next few years to encourage a strong and healthy language development.

ACTIVITY – Place the materials on the floor between yourself and your baby. Let your baby explore the materials first, touching each item while you talk about what they are seeing and doing (parallel talk). Once you feel your baby has sufficiently explored the objects, sit the teddy bear up and tell your baby that he is hungry! Explain that you should feed the teddy then pick up the bowl and spoon and start mixing the pretend food, then pretend to feed the teddy with the spoon. Try to feed the teddy three times while your baby watches before offering them a turn feeding the teddy too.

MY BABY WILL – Take the spoon then imitate my action of putting the spoon to the teddy's mouth to "feed" him.

THEN I WILL – Say, "Oh teddy is so hungry! Good job feeding teddy". I will make eating noises each time either I, or my baby, feeds the teddy (e.g., "yum, yum, yum"). If my baby does not imitate my actions I will try to gently physically prompt them to copy me.

TIP

Make sure the room you are playing in is free from distractions so your baby can concentrate on playing with you. Don't be discouraged if they do not imitate you immediately. Pretending is a skill that develops over time, so just continue to practice each day and they will soon be eager to join in the game.

DAILY TALKING GAMES

- Jolly Jump – Hold your baby's hands and help them jump on the sofa, then stop and wait.

- Swing 'N Talk – Start pushing your baby on the swing, then pause and wait before pushing again.

- Family Trail – Tape a few family pictures to the floor then encourage your baby to explore the photos with you, pausing at each picture.

- Bouncing Horsey Ride – Bounce your baby up and down on your knee then stop and wait after a few bounces.

- Toy Hide-and-Seek – Hide a toy around the room, let your baby look for the toy, then wait expectantly after they have found it.

- Phone Time – Use two pretend phones (one for your baby and one for you), then "call" your baby on their phone to talk.

- Tickle Time – Give your baby lots of tickles then stop and wait, holding your hands up expectantly, before tickling again.

All daily talking games should include pauses, or expectant waiting, to give your baby a chance to add a sound or word into the game too.

WORD TOSS CATEGORY IDEAS

Some ideas could include:
- food
- vehicles
- animals
- clothing
- tools
- dishes
- plants
- people
- shoes
- birds
- instruments

SIMPLE PRETEND PLAY

Ideas you might try:
- put a blanket on a doll or teddy before they go to sleep
- give a doll or teddy a drink
- have a doll or teddy eat some pretend food
- pretend to talk on a toy phone
- drive a toy car or other vehicle
- wash a doll or teddy with a cloth
- pretend to cook by stirring a spoon in a bowl
- pour a pretend drink in a cup
- kiss or hug a doll or teddy to make them "feel better"
- brush a teddy's or doll's teeth

12 MONTH MILESTONES AND MEMORIES

Congratulations! You have helped your baby learn how to communicate since the very first moment they were born, and they are now ready to start talking. With your help, here is what your baby can do now:

	Understanding Language	**Using Language**
9 to 12 Months	Understands between 3-50 words	Uses gestures to communicate (e.g., points to desired items, waves, etc.)
	Enjoys songs and rhymes	Imitates different speech sounds
	Responds by looking at what an adult is pointing to	Uses a variety of consonant sounds in jargon, babbling or words
	Responds to simple requests (e.g., come here, give me the…)	Makes vocalizations during play when alone and when playing with an adult
	Engages in cause and effect play	

Here are all the things you are now doing each day to help them prepare to become confident communicators:

Offering opportunities for my baby to help in daily routines by following simple directions	Observing my baby's non-verbal gestures and interpreting the communicative message my baby is trying to send me	Repeating words during simple play routines together
Offering a choice of two items at meals to encourage word use	Using the Rule of Thumb is 5:1 – five comments and one question during storybook reading together	Encouraging imitation of sounds in play
Setting up some simple sabotage in daily routines to encourage talking	Playing games to develop social language like "hi" and "bye"	Pausing in familiar songs to encourage my baby to use sounds and words
Playing a daily talking game for five minutes	Playing category games that broaden my baby's vocabulary knowledge	Engaging in simple pretend play with my baby

12 MONTH MILESTONES AND MEMORIES

PUT A PICTURE OF YOUR BABY HERE

My baby's favourite books are:
_____
_____
_____
_____

Games my baby likes to play are:
_____
_____
_____
_____

Songs my baby enjoys are:
_____
_____
_____
_____

Nursery rhymes my baby likes to listen to are:
_____
_____
_____
_____

My baby's favourite outings include:
___

Things my baby likes to play with are:
___

The daily talking game we do is:
___

My baby's first word was:
___

Over the next year I am going to continue to help my baby become a confident communicator by:
___

WORD TRACKER

Keep track of your baby's growing vocabulary using the chart below. Each time you hear your baby use a new word, add it to the list!

Date	Nouns	Verbs	Prepositions	Pronouns	Adjectives	Other

FINAL THOUGHTS

At this point we have come to the end of your baby's language learning journey for their first year. Your role in this process cannot be understated. You have been there each step of the way, supporting, guiding, teaching and loving your baby as they have progressed on their own unique and special journey into the world of talking.

I encourage you to take a few minutes and go back through this book to remind yourself just how much you have learned and how far you, and your baby, have come in this first year as parent and child together.

Going forward into the next year you can feel confident that you have given your baby the very best start in their language development. I urge you to continue the activities suggested in this book, modifying each one as needed, to match your baby's developing language skills. I also recommend using the resource lists provided to learn more about how you can continue to support your child's language learning in the toddler years and beyond. There is also a chart at the end of the book on p.133 that can be used as a guideline for what to expect over the next year in your baby's language development.

I would like to end with a big congratulations to your family, your baby and of course, to you. Together you have completed the first year in the journey from birth to first words.

APPENDIX

TROUBLE SHOOTING STRATEGIES

Here are some questions to ask yourself if your baby is not responding as expected to the activities suggested in this book.

1) **Have all my baby's behavioural needs been satisfied?**
   Babies need to feel content before they are ready to engage with another person. This means they are not hungry, tired, in any pain or discomfort before or during the activity.

2) **Does this activity work with my baby's unique personality?**
   Each baby is different and this needs to be taken into consideration during interactions. Think about your baby's personality (e.g., shy, outgoing, cautious, adventurous, etc.) and see if you need to modify the activity to fit your baby's style.

3) **Are there other distractions in the environment?**
   Observe what is happening around you that may affect the quality of the interaction with your baby. For example, is the television on, are there background noises from other sources, or are there other people or other objects/toys that are distracting your baby from the interaction with you?

4) **Is this the first time you have tried the activity?**
   Some of these activities require familiarization on the part of both the adult and the baby for them to be effective. Practicing each day is very important, as well as continuing to maintain the other activities previously learned since each skill builds on the next.

5) **Are you having fun too?**
   This may seem silly, but babies can tell if an adult is enjoying themselves during an interaction. They look at faces and are more likely to engage with a person that is smiling, making eye contact and generally having fun. Remember, what you bring to the activity is just as important as the activity itself.

6) **Do you have the correct materials?**
   Although there is lots of flexibility with these activities, allowing you to choose different materials based on your baby's interests and what you have available at home, they are based around the recommended items for optimal effectiveness.

7) **Have you asked someone else in your family?**
   Along with yourself, members of your family know your baby best. If you are having trouble with any activity ask another family member to read the activity and attempt to complete it themselves. Discuss possible reasons your baby may not be responding as expected and problem solve together.

RESOURCES

Books

Beyond Baby Talk by Kenn Apel and Julie Masterson

How Babies Talk: The Magic and Mystery of Language in the First Three Years of Life by Dr. Roberta Michnick Golinkoff and Dr. Kathy Hirsh-Pasek

The Scientist in the Crib by Dr. Alison Gopnik, Dr. Andrew N. Meltzoff and Dr. Patricia K. Kuhl

Small Talk: Simple Ways To Boost Your Child's Speech and Language Development From Birth by Nicola Lathey and Tracey Blake

Let's Talk Together: Home Activities for Early Speech & Language Development by Amy Chouinard and Cory Poland

Websites

http://kidcarecanada.org

http://www.wordsforlife.org.uk

http://www.talkingpoint.org.uk

https://www.zerotothree.org

http://www.readingrockets.org

REGULATORY BODIES FOR SPEECH-LANGUAGE PATHOLOGISTS AND AUDIOLOGISTS

Speech-Language & Audiology Canada
https://www.sac-oac.ca

American Speech-Language-Hearing Association
https://www.asha.org

Speech Pathology Australia
https://www.speechpathologyaustralia.org.au

Royal College of Speech and Language Therapists – UK
https://www.rcslt.org

The Irish Association of Speech & Language Therapists
http://www.iaslt.ie

New Zealand Speech-language Therapists' Association
https://speechtherapy.org.nz

WHAT TO EXPECT IN THE NEXT YEAR

As your baby progresses over the next year you should see these skills emerge. By the time your baby has their second birthday they should be exhibiting all the language abilities listed below.

	Understanding Language	**Using Language**
12 – 24 Months	Understands approximately 50-300 words by 18 months	Uses at least 20 words by 18 months
	Follows one-step directions (e.g., kiss the baby, pick up the book)	Uses one-word phrases to communicate and moves into using two-word phrases by 24 months
	Identifies some simple body parts (e.g., nose, tummy, head)	Makes eye contact during communication
	Understands basic yes/no questions	Uses raising intonation to ask yes/no questions
	Understands simple 'wh' questions such as what, where and who	Says more words every month and tries to imitate new words
	Identifies common or familiar objects in a book	Engages in approximately five communicative acts per minute during play with an adult
	Understands words for objects out of sight	Vocabulary includes nouns, verbs, social words and rejection words
	Engages in simple symbolic play (e.g., pretends to feed a doll)	Directs an adult's attention to look at something
	Listens to stories, songs and rhymes for increasingly longer periods of time	Initiates turn-taking games with an adult (e.g., rolling a ball)

WHAT TO DO IF YOU HAVE CONCERNS ABOUT YOUR CHILD'S LANGUAGE DEVELOPMENT

Although most children will start talking around their first birthday, there are others that may need a little extra support. Here are a few suggestions for what to do if you feel your baby's language skills may not be on track:

- Speak to your child's doctor about what you are thinking. They have been monitoring your baby's health over the past year and should be able to answer many of your questions or make referrals if necessary.

- Disruptions to hearing are common in the early years of life and may affect speech and language development in the short-term. Having your baby checked by an audiologist to ensure proper hearing health is a good first step to ensure your baby's language development stays on track.

- Many speech-language pathologists are happy to answer questions from parents who have concerns. Use the list provided in this book to find a speech and language pathologist in your country.

- Use the resource list in this book to learn more about what to expect in your baby's early language development and how to encourage growing language skills at home.

- Take the pressure off talking. Babies do not like to be asked to repeat words often or to be tested with questions. One of the best ways to encourage talking is to provide your baby with regular daily interactions with you that are based on their unique interests, are fun and offer lots of back-and-forth turns while you play together.

KEY TERMS

Babbling – A series of reduplicated consonant-vowel combinations that have the same sounds repeated in clear syllables.

Cooing – Vowel-like sounds that babies produce around 2-3 months of age, generally when they are engaging with an adult and are happy and content.

Early literacy – Skills and knowledge children acquire before learning to read and write, such as how to hold a book, turn pages, engaging with reading materials appropriately, awareness that print on the page contains information and enjoyment of reading.

Expressive language – A part of language characterized by the use of sounds, words and sentences to communicate a message with another person.

Fast mapping – A theoretical way young children develop vocabulary by quickly attaching a new word they hear to an action or an object in their environment to establish meaning for that word.

First word – A word that is produced with the intention of sending a message to another person, that is used with consistent meaning and is a close approximation to the actual word as would be said by an adult.

Infant-directed speech – A way of speaking to an infant that includes using a higher pitch, elongated vowel sounds, exaggerated pitch contours, more pauses between phrases and repetition of words and short phrases.

Joint attention – When two people are looking at the same object or event at the same time and both are aware that the other is seeing the same thing.

Non-reduplicated babbling – When babies produce repeated sequences of different consonants and vowel combinations as syllables.

Parallel talk - A technique in which the adult describes what the child is doing or seeing without expecting a response.

Phonological development – The process of learning all the sounds and the sound patterns needed for the use of that language.

Pragmatic language – The use of verbal and non-verbal behaviour, such as eye contact, body language and facial expression, used to communicate messages between people.

Prosody – The changes to intonation that occur while speaking, such as variations in pitch and stress.

Protoword – A word that a young child uses to communicate that has consistent meaning but is not found in the language they are learning.

Receptive language – A part of language characterized by the understanding of sound, word and sentence meanings that have been spoken by another person.

Self-talk - A strategy in which the adult uses words to describe their own actions without expecting the child to respond.

Vocabulary – The dictionary of words, and their associated knowledge, that people have in their minds for a specific language or languages.

Vocal play – When infants produce various speech and non-speech sounds, typically occurring between 4-6 months of age.

REFERENCES

Letter From The Author

Apel, K. & Masterson, J. *Beyond Baby Talk: From Speaking to Spelling: A Guide to Language and Literacy Development for Parents and Caregivers.* New York, NY: Three Rivers Press, 2012.

Aro, T., Laakso, M., Maatta, S., Tolvanen, A., & Poikkeus, A. (2014). Associations between toddler-age communication and kindergarten-age self-regulatory skills. *Journal of Speech, Language, and Hearing Research*, 57 (4), 1405-1417.

Bonci, A., Mottram, E., McCoy, E., & Cole, J. (2011). *A research review: the importance of families and the home environment.* National Literacy Trust Report.

Chapman, R. S. (2000). Children's language learning: An interactionist perspective. *Journal of Child Psychology and Psychiatry, 41(1),* 33-54.

Conti-Ramsden, G., Durkin, K., Toseeb, U., Botting, N., & Pickles, A. (2017). Education and employment outcomes of young adults with a history of developmental language disorder. *International Journal of Language and Communication Disorders,* 1-19.

Einarsdottir, J. T., Bjornsdottir, A., & Simonardottir, I. (2016). The predictive value of preschool language assessments on academic achievement: A 10-year longitudinal study of Icelandic children. *American Journal of Speech-Language Pathology,* 1-13.

Gopnick, A., Meltzoff, A. N. & Kuhl, P. K. *The Scientist In The Crib: What Early Learning Tells Us About The Mind.* New York: NY: Harper Perennial, 1999.

Hoff, E. *Language Development, 5th Ed..* Belmont, CA: Wadsworth, 2014.

Hoff, E. (2006). How social contexts support and shape language development. *Developmental Review, 26,* 55-88.

Yu, M., & Daraganova, G. (2014). *Children's early home learning environment and learning outcomes in the early years of school.* LSAC Annual Statistical Report.

Yurovsky, D., A communicative approach to early word learning, New Ideas in Psychology (2017), http:// dx.doi.org/10.1016/j.newideapsych.2017.09.001.

Newborn

Bell, S., & Ainsworth, M. (1972). Infant crying and maternal responsiveness. *Child Development, 43,* 1171-1190.

Dunst, C. J., Simkus, A., & Hamby, D. W., (2012). Effects of reading to infants and toddlers on their early language development. *Center For Early Literacy Learning Reviews, 5(4),* 1-7.

Dunst, C. J., Simkus, A., & Hamby, D. W., (2012). Relationship between age of onset and frequency of reading and infants' and toddlers' early language and literacy development. *Center For Early Literacy Learning Reviews, 5(3),* 1-10.

Gervain, J. (2015). Plasticity in early language acquisition: the effects of prenatal and early childhood experience. *Current Opinion in Neurobiology, 35,* 13-20.

Golinkoff, R. M., & Hirsh-Pasek, K. *How Babies Talk: The Magic and Mystery of Language in the First Three Years of Life.* New York, NY: Plume Publishing, 1999, p. 20-21.

Hoff, E. *Language Development, 5th ed.* Belmont, CA: Wadsworth, 2014, p. 87-89.

Trainor, L. J. (1996). Infant preferences for infant-directed versus noninfant-directed playsongs and lullabies. *Infant Behavior and Development, 19,* 83-92.

Vihman, M. M. (2017). Learning words and learning sounds: Advances in language development. *British Journal of Psychology, 108(1),* 1-27.

1 Month Old

American Academy of Pediatrics. *The Wonder Years,* New York, NY: Bantam Books, 2006.

Brazelton, T. B., & Cramer, B. G. *The Earliest Relationships: Parents, Infants and the Drama of Early Attachment,* Cambridge, MA: DaCapo Press, 1990.

Bowen, C. (2011). Table4: Phonetic Development. Retrieved from http://www.speech-language-therapy.com/ on February 19, 2019.

Cooper, R., & Aslin, R. N. (1990). Preference for infant-directed speech in the first month after birth. *Child Development, 61,* 1584-1595.

Golinkoff, R. M., & Hirsh-Pasek, K. *How Babies Talk: The Magic and Mystery of Language in the First Three Years of Life.* New York, NY: Plume Publishing, 1999, p. 30.

Lathey, N. & Blake, T. *Small talk: Simple ways to boost your child's speech and language development from birth.* London, U.K.: Macmillan, 2013.

Ma, W., Golinkoff, R. M., Houston, D., & Hirsh-Pasek, K. (2011). Word learning in infant and adult-directed speech. *Language Learning and Development, 7,* 209-225.

March of Dimes. (2003). Understanding the behaviour of term infants. *Perinatal Nursing Education,* 1-14.

Meltzoff, A. N. "Born to learn: What infants learn from watching us." In *The Role of Early Experience in Infant Development,* edited by N. Fox & J.G. Worhol, Skillman, NJ: Pediatric Institute Publications, 1999.

Pascalis, O. Loevenbruck, H., Quinn, P. C., Kandel, S., Tanaka, J. W., & Lee, K. (2014). On the links among face processing, language processing and narrowing during development. *Child Development Perspectives, 8(2),* 65-70.

Trainor, L. J. & Desjardins, R. (2002). Pitch characteristics of infant-directed speech affect infants' ability to discriminate vowels. *Psychonomic Bulletin and Review, 9(2),* 335-340.

2 Months Old

Apel, K. & Masterson, J. *Beyond Baby Talk: From Speaking to Spelling: A Guide to Language and Literacy Development for Parents and Caregivers.* New York, NY: Three Rivers Press, 2012, p. 22-31.

Golinkoff, R.M., Deniz Can, D., Soderstrom, M., & Hirsh-Pasek, K. (2015). (Baby) Talk to me: The social context of infant-directed speech and its effects on early language acquisition. *Current Directions in Psychological Science, 24(5),* 339-344.

Gopnick, A., Meltzoff, A. N. & Kuhl, P. K. *The Scientist In The Crib: What Early Learning Tells Us About The Mind.* New York: NY: Harper Perennial, 1999.

Graf-Estes, K. Chen-Wu Gluck, S., & Grimm, K. J. (2016). Finding patterns and learning words: Infant phonotactic knowledge is associated with vocabulary size. *Journal of Experimental Child Psychology, 146,* 34-49.

Gratier, M., Devouche, E., Guellai, B., Infanti, R., Yilmaz, E., & Parlato-Oliveira, E. (2015). Early development of turn-taking in vocal interaction between mothers and infants. *Frontiers in Psychology*, doi: 10.3389/fpsyg.2015.01167.

Hoff, E. *Language Development, 5th ed*. Belmont, CA: Wadsworth, 2014, p. 83, 87-89, 111.

Lavelli, M. & Fogel, A. (2005). Developmental changes in the relationship between the infant's attention and emotion during early face-to-face communication: The 2-month transition. *Developmental Psychology, 41(1),* 265-280.

Sanes, D. H. & Bao, S. (2009). Tuning up the developing auditory CNS. *Current Opinions in Neurobiology, 19(20),* 188-199.

Swingley, D. (2008). The roots of the early vocabulary in infants' learning from speech. *Current Directions in Psychological Science, 17(5),* 308-311.

3 Months Old

Bourvis, N., Singer, M., Saint Georges, C., Bodeau, N., Chetouani, M., Cohen, D., & Feldman, R. (2018). Pre-linguistic infants employ complex communicative loops to engage mothers in social exchanges and repair interaction ruptures. *Royal Society Open Science, 5(170274),* 1-14.

Fantasia, V., Fasulo, A., Costall, A. & Lopez, B. (2014). Changing the game: exploring infants' participation in early play routines. *Frontiers in Psychology, 5,* 1-9.

Golinkoff, R. M., & Hirsh-Pasek, K. *How Babies Talk: The Magic and Mystery of Language in the First Three Years of Life*. New York, NY: Plume Publishing, 1999, p. 27-28.

Harder, S., Lange, T., Hansen, G. F., Vaever, M., & Koppe, S. (2015). A longitudinal study of coordination in mother-infant vocal interaction from age 4 to 10 months. *Developmental Psychology*. Advance online publication. http://dx.doi.org/10.1037/a0039834.

Hoff, E. (2006). How social contexts support and shape language development. *Developmental Review, 26,* 55-88.

Kuhl, P. K. & Meltzoff, A. N. (1996). Infant vocalizations in response to speech: Vocal imitation and developmental change. *The Journal of the Acoustical Society of America, 100*(4 Pt 1), 2425-2438.

Meltzoff, A. N. "Imitation and Other Minds: The "Like Me" Hypothesis." In *Perspective on Imitation: From Neuroscience to Social Science*, edited by S. Hurley and N. Chater, Cambridge, MA: MIT Press, 2005.

Meltzoff, A. N. & Moore, K. M. (1992). Early imitation within a functional framework: The importance of person identity, movement and development. *Infant Behavior and Development, 15(4),* 479-505.

Mundy, P. & Jarrold, W. (2010). Infant joint attention, neural networks and social cognition. *Neural Networks, 23(8-9),* 985-997.

Ruvolo, P., Messinger, D. & Movellan, J. (2015). Infants time their smiles to make their moms smile. *PLoS ONE, 10(9):* e0136492. doi:10.1371/ journal.pone.0136492.

4 Months Old

Goldstein, J. *Play in Children's Development, Health and Well-being*. Brussels, Belgium: Toy Industries of Europe, 2012.

Goldstein, M. H., Schwade, J. A. & Bornstein, M. H. (2009). The value of vocalizing: Five-month-old infants associate their noncry vocalizations with responses from caregivers. *Child Development, 80(3),* 636-644.

Hart, B. & Risley, T. R. *The Social World of Children Learning To Talk*. Baltimore: MD: Paul H. Brookes Publishing Company, 1999.

Hart, B., & Risley, T. R. *Meaningful differences in the everyday experience of young American children*. Baltimore, MD: Paul H. Brookes Publishing Company, 1995.

Hoff, E. *Language Development, 5th ed.*. Belmont, CA: Wadsworth, 2014, p. 116-117, 119-120.

Masapollo, M., Polka, L., & Menard, L. (2016). When infants talk, infants listen: pre-babbling infants prefer listening to speech with infant vocal properties. *Developmental Science, 19(2),* 318-328.

Mireault, G. C., Crockenberg, S. C., Sparrow, J. E., Cousineau, K., Pettinato, C. & Woodard, K. (2015). Laughing matters: infant humour in the context of parental affect. *Journal of Experimental Child Psychology, 136,* 30-41.

Mireault, G., Poutre, M., Sargent-Hier, M., Dias, C., Perdue, B. & Myrick, A. (2011). Humour perception and creation between parents and 3 – to 6-month old infants. *Infant and Child Development, 21(4),* 338-347.

Rvachew, S., & Alhaidary, A. (2018). The Phonetics of Babbling. *Oxford Research Encyclopedia of Linguistics*. Retrieved 10 May. 2018, from http://linguistics.oxfordre.com/view/10.1093/acrefore/9780199384655.001.0001/acrefore-9780199384655-e-413.

5 Months Old

Hedenbro, M. & Rydelius, P. (2013). Early interaction between infants and their parents predicts social competence at the age of four. *Foundation Acta Paediatrica, 103,* p. 268-274.

Hilbrink, E. E., Gattis, M. & Levinson, S. C. (2015). Early developmental changes in the timing of turn-taking: a longitudinal study of mother-infant interaction. *Frontiers in Psychology, 6:1492,* doi: 10.3389/fpsyg.2015.01492.

Hoff, E. (2006). How social contexts support and shape language development. *Developmental Review, 26,* 55-88.

Hoff, E. *Language Development, 5th Ed.*. Belmont, CA: Wadsworth, 2014, p. 146.

Nomikou, I., Leonardi, G, Radkowska, A., Raczaszek-Leonardi, J. & Rohlfing, K. J. (2017). Taking up an active role: Emerging participation in early mother-infant interaction during peek-a-boo routine. *Frontiers in Psychology 8:1656.* doi: 10.3389/fpsyg.2017.01656.

Özçaliskan, S. & Dimitrova, N. (2013). How gesture input provides a helping hand to language development. *Seminars in Speech and Language, 34(4)*, 227-236.

Rowe, M. L. (2017). Understanding socioeconomic differences in parents' speech to children. *Child Development Perspectives,* 1-6.

Rowe, M. L. & Goldin-Meadow, S. (2009). Differences in early gesture explain SES disparities in child vocabulary size at school entry. *Science, 323,* 951-953.

Tamis-LeMonda, C. S., Kuchirko, Y. & Song, L. (2014). Why is infant language learning facilitated by parental responsiveness? *Current Directions in Psychological Science, 23,* 121-126.

6 Months Old

B.M. Maas, A. J., Vreeswijk, C. M. J. M., & Van Bakel, H. J. A. (2013). Effect of situation on mother-infant interaction. *Infant Behavior and Development, 36,* 42-49.

Barr, R., Vieira, A. & Rovee-Collier, C. (2001). Mediated imitation in 6-month-olds: Remembering by association. *Journal of Experimental Child Psychology, 79,* 229-252.

Carpenter, M. "Instrumental, social and shared goals and intentions in imitation." In *Imitation and the Social Mind: Autism and Typical Development,* edited by S. J. Rogers & J.H.G. Williams, New York: NY: Guilford Press, 2006.

Duursma, E., Augustyn, M. & Zuckerman, B. (2008). Reading aloud to children: the evidence. *Archives of Disease in Childhood, 93(7),* 554-557.

Goldstein, M. H. & Schwade, J. A. (2088). Social feedback to infants' babbling facilitates rapid phonological learning. *Psychological Science, 19(5),* 515-523.

Hamer, C. (2012). NCT research overview: Parent-child communication is important from birth. *Perspective,* 15-20.

High, P. C., LaGasse, L., Becker, S., Ahlgren, I. & Gardner, A. (2000). Literacy promotion in primary care pediatrics: Can we make a difference? *Pediatrics, 105(4),* 927-934.

Hoff, E. *Language Development, 5th ed.* Belmont, CA: Wadsworth, 2014, p. 117, 121.

Learmonth, A. E., Cueva, K. & Rovee-Collier, C. (2105). Deconstructing the reactivation of imitation in young infants. *Developmental Psychobiology, 57(4),* 497-505.

Oller, D. K., Eilers, R. E., Neal, A. R. & Schwartz, H. K. (1999). Precursors to speech in infancy: the prediction of speech and language disorders. *Journal of Communication Disorders 32(4),* 223-245.

Olswang, L. B., Rodriguez, B. & Timler, G. (1998). Recommending interventions for toddlers with specific language learning difficulties: We may not have all the answers but we know a lot. *American Journal of Speech-Language Pathology, 7(1),* 23-32.

7 Months Old

Bergelson, E. & Swingley, D. (2012). At 6-9 months, human infants know the meanings of many common nouns. *PNAS.org, 109(9),* 3253-3258.

Dunst, C. J., Gorman, E. & Hamby, D. W. (2010). Effects of adult verbal and vocal contingent responsiveness on increases in infant vocalization. *Center For Early Literacy Learning Reviews, 3(1),* 1-11.

Gambell, Timothy & Yang, Charles. (2005). Word segmentation: Quick but not dirty. Retrieved online on April 18, 2019 at https://www.ling.upenn.edu/~ycharles/papers/quick.pdf.

Hart, B., & Risley, T. R. *Meaningful differences in the everyday experience of young American children.* Baltimore, MD: Paul H. Brookes Publishing Company, 1995.

Marchman, V. A. & Fernald, A. (2008). Speed of word recognition and vocabulary knowledge in infancy predict cognitive and language outcomes in later childhood. *Developmental Science, 11(3),* 9-16.

Rowe, M. L. (2012). A longitudinal investigation of the role of quantity and quality of child-directed speech in vocabulary development. *Child Development, 83(5),* 1762-1774.

Singh, L., Reznick, J. S. & Xuehua, L. (2012). Infant word segmentation and childhood vocabulary development: A longitudinal analysis. *Developmental Science, 15(4),* 482-495.

Sonderegger, M. (2008). Infant word segmentation: a basic review. Retrieved online on March 28, 2018 at people.cs.uchicago.edu/~morgan/segReview.pdf.

Suskind, D. *Thirty Million Words: Building A Child's Brain.* New York, NY: Dutton, 2015.

Weisleder, A. & Fernald, A. (2013). Talking to children matters: early language experience strengthens processing and builds vocabulary. *Psychological Science, 24(11),* 2143-2152.

8 Months Old

American Academy of Pediatrics. *Handheld screen time linked with speech delays in young children.* Retrieved online on April 5, 2018 at http://www.aappublications.org/news/2017/05/04/PASScreenTime050417.

Canadian Peadiatric Society. (2107). Screen time and young children: Promoting health and development in a digital world. *Peadiatrics and Child Health, 22(8),* 461-468.

Gunn, B. K., Simmons, D. C. & Kameenui, E. J. Emergent literacy: Synthesis of the research. Retrieved online on May 28, 2018 at https://pdfs.semanticscholar.org/0726/4f9b6bca66d3b9bdc9ee95f069c1a4c02dd9.pdf.

Hoff, E. (2006). How social contexts support and shape language development. *Developmental Review, 26,* 55-88.

Horst, J. S. (2013). Context and repetition in word learning. *Frontiers in Psychology, 4(149),* 1-11.

Liszkowski, U. (2014). Two sources of meaning in infant communication: preceding action contexts and act-accompanying characteristics. *Philosophical Transactions of the Royal Society, 369,* 20130294. http://dx.doi.org/10.1098/rstb.2013.0294.

Meltzoff, A. N. "Imitation and Other Minds: The "Like Me" Hypothesis." In *Perspective on Imitation: From Neuroscience to Social Science,* edited by S. Hurley and N. Chater, Cambridge, MA: MIT Press, 2005.

Newman, R. S., Rowe, M. L. & Bernstein Ratner, N. (2016). Input and uptake at 7 months predicts toddler vocabulary: the role of child-directed speech and infant processing skills in language development. *Journal of Child Language, 43,* 1158-1173.

Spedding, S., Harkins, J., Makin, L. & Whiteman, P. (2007). *Investigating children's early literacy learning in family and community contexts: Review of the related literature.* Adelaide, SA: Department of Education and Children's Services.

Zimmerman, F. J., Christakis, D. A., & Meltzoff, A. N. (2007). Associations between media viewing and language development in children under age 2 years. *Journal of Pediatrics, 151(4),* 364-368.

9 Months Old

Apel, K. & Masterson, J. *Beyond Baby Talk: From Speaking to Spelling: A Guide to Language and Literacy Development for Parents and Caregivers.* New York, NY: Three Rivers Press, 2012, p. 22-31.

Beuker, K. T., Rommelse, N. N. J., Donders, R. & Buitelaar, J. K. (2013). Development of early communication skills in the first two years of life. *Infant Behavior and Development, 36,* 71-83.

Duursma, E., Augustyn, M. & Zuckerman, B. (2008). Reading aloud to children: the evidence. *Archives of Disease in Childhood, 93(7),* 554-557.

Gong, T. Shuai, L. (2012). Modeling the coevolution of joint attention and language. *Proceedings of The Royal Society, 279,* 4643-4651.

Gros-Louis, J., West, M. J., & King, A. P. (2014). Maternal responsiveness and the development of directed vocalizing in social interactions. *Infancy,* 1-24.

High, P. C., LaGasse, L., Becker, S., Ahlgren, I. & Gardner, A. (2000). Literacy promotion in primary care pediatrics: Can we make a difference? *Pediatrics, 105(4),* 927-934.

Hoff, E. *Language Development, 5th ed.* Belmont, CA: Wadsworth, 2014, p. 119 -120.

Luke, C., Grimminger, A., Rohlfing, K. J., & Liszkowski, Ulf. (2017). In infants' hands: Identification of preverbal infants at risk for primary language delay. *Child Development, 88(2),* 484-492.

Montag. J. L., Jones, M. N. & Smith, L. B. (2018). Quantity and diversity: Stimulating early word learning environments. *Cognitive Science,* 1-38.

Senechal, M. & LeFevre, J. (2002). Parental involvement in the development of children's reading skill: a five-year longitudinal study. *Child Development, 73,* 445-460.

Swigert, N. B. *The Early Intervention Kit.* East Moline, IL: Linguisystems, 2014.

Vaughan Van Hecke, A., Mundy, P., Block, J. J., Delgado, C. E. F., Parlade, M. V., Pomares, Y. B. & Hobson, J. A. (2012). Infant responding to joint attention, executive processes and self-regulation in preschool children. *Infant Behavior and Development, 35(2),* 303-311.

10 Months Old

Boundy, L., Cameron-Faulkner, T., & Theakston. (2016). Exploring early communicative behaviours: A fine-grained analysis of infant shows and gives. *Infant Behavior and Development, 44,* 86-97.

Capone, N. C., McGregor, K. K. (2004). Gesture development: A review for clinical and research practices. *Journal of Speech, Language and Hearing Research, 47,* 173-186.

Colonnesi, C., J.M. Stams, J. G., Koster, I. & Noom, M. J. (2010). The relation between pointing and language development: A meta-analysis. *Developmental Review, 30,* 352-366.

Fenson, L, Dale, P. S., Reznick, J. S., Bates, E., Thal, D. J., & Pethick, S. J. (1994). Variability in early communicative development. *Monographs of the Society for Research in Child Development, 59(5),* 1-173.

Hoff, E. (2006). How social contexts support and shape language development. *Developmental Review, 26,* 55-88.

Hoff, E. *Language Development, 5th ed..* Belmont, CA: Wadsworth, 2014, p. 139, 147.

Newman, R. S., Rowe, M. L. & Bernstein Ratner, N. (2016). Input and uptake at 7 months predicts toddler vocabulary: the role of child-directed speech and infant processing skills in language development. *Journal of Child Language, 43,* 1158-1173.

Pruden, S. M., Hirsh-Pasek, K., Golinkoff, R. M. & Hennon, E. A. (2006). The birth of words: ten-month-olds learn words through perceptual salience. *Child Development, 77(2),* 266-280.

Rowe, M. L. & Goldin-Meadow, S. (2009). Early gesture selectively predicts later language learning. *Developmental Science, 12(1),* 182-187.

Roy, B. C., Frank, M. C., DeCamp, P., Miller, M. & Roy, D. (2015). Predicting the birth of a spoken word. *PNAS Early Edition,* doi/10.1073/pnas.1419773112.

Swigert, N. B. *The Early Intervention Kit.* East Moline, IL: Linguisystems, 2014.

Tamis-LeMonda, C. S., Custode, S., Kuchirko, Y., Escobar, K., & Lo, T. (2018). Routine language: speech directed to infants during home activities. *Child Development,* doi:10.1111/cdev.13089.

11 Months Old

Frank Masur, E., & Olson, J. (2008). Mothers' and infants' responses to their partners' spontaneous action and vocal/verbal imitation. *Infant Behavior and Development, 31(4),* 704-715.

Goldstein, M. H., Schwade, J., Briesch, J., & Syal, S. (2010). Learning while babbling: Prelinguistic object-directed vocalizations indicate a readiness to learn. *Infancy, 15(4),* 362-391.

Gunn, B. K., Simmons, D. C. & Kameenui, E. J. *Emergent Literacy: Synthesis of the research.* Eugene, OR: National Center To Improve the Tools of Educators, 1995.

Hoff, E. *Language Development, 5th ed..* Belmont, CA: Wadsworth, 2014, p. 139, 147.

Lathey, N. & Blake, T. *Small talk: Simple ways to boost your child's speech and language development from birth.* London, U.K.: Macmillan, 2013.

Pepper, J., & Weitzman, E. *It Takes Two To Talk.* Toronto, ON: The Hanen Centre, 2004.

Strid, K., Tjus, T., Smith, L., Meltzoff, A. N., & Heimann, M. (2006). Infant recall memory and communication predicts later cognitive development. *Infant Behavior and Development, 29,* 545-553.

Zimmerman, F. J., Gilkerson, J, Richards, J. A., Christakis, D. A., Xu, D., Gray, S., & Yapanel, U. (2009). Teaching by listening: The importance of adult-child conversations to language development. *Pediatrics, 124(1),* 342-349.

12 Months Old

Apel, K. & Masterson, J. *Beyond Baby Talk: From Speaking to Spelling: A Guide to Language and Literacy Development for Parents and Caregivers.* New York, NY: Three Rivers Press, 2012, p. 22-31.

Biro, S. & Leslie, A. M. (2007). Infants' perception of goal-directed actions: development through cue-based bootstrapping. *Developmental Science, 10(3),* 379-398.

Ferguson, B., Havy, M., & Waxman, S. R. (2015). The precision of 12-month-old infants' link between language and categorization predicts vocabulary size at 12 and 18 months. *Frontiers in Psychology, 6(1319),* 1-6.

Fulkerson, A. L. & Waxman, S. R. (2007). Words (but not tones) facilitate object categorization: evidence from 6- and 12-month-olds. *Cognition, 105(1),* 218-228.

Leong, V. Byrne, E., Clackson, K., Georgieva, S., Lam, S., Wass, S. (2017). Speaker gaze increases information coupling between infant and adult brains. *PNAS, 114(50),* 13290-13295.

Mani, N. & Ackermann, L. (2018). Why do children learn the words they do? *Child Development Perspectives,* 1-5.

Orr, E. & Geva, R. (2015). Symbolic play and language development. *Infant Behavior and Development, 38,* 147-161.

Vihman, M. M. (2016). Learning words and learning sounds: Advances in language development. *British Journal of Psychology, 108(1),* 1-27.

Waxman, S. & Booth, A. (2003). The origins and evolution of links between word learning and conceptual organization: new evidence from 11-month olds. *Developmental Science, 6(2),* 128-135.

Waxman, S. R. & Lidz, J. (2006). Early word learning. In D. Kuhn & R. Siegler (Eds.), *Handbook of Child Psychology,* 6th Edition, Volume 2.

Yin, J. & Csibra, G. (2015). Concept-based word learning in human infants. *Psychological Science, 26(8),* 1316-1324.

Milestone Charts

American Speech and Hearing Association (n.d.). *How Does Your Child Hear and Talk?* Retrieved online on April 7, 2016 at http://www.asha.org/public/speech/development/chart/.

Apel, K. & Masterson, J. *Beyond Baby Talk: From Speaking to Spelling: A Guide to Language and Literacy Development for Parents and Caregivers.* New York, NY: Three Rivers Press, 2012.

Paul, R. *Language Disorders From Infancy Through Adolescence: Assessment and Intervention,* 3rd ed. New Haven, CT: Mosby Elsevier, 2007.

Sax, N. & Weston, E. (2007). Language Development Milestones. Retrieved online on May 11, 2016 at http://www.rehabmed.ualberta.ca/spa/phonology/milestones.pdf.

Speech Pathology and Audiology Canada (n.d.) *Speech, Language and Hearing Milestones*. Retrieved online on February 6, 2018 at https://www.sac-oac.ca/sites/default/files/resources/SAC-Milestones-TriFold_EN.pdf.

PICTURE REFERENCES

Page 9   Bathe newborn, image ID: 53920289, Luca Lorenzelli.

Page 10   Young woman reading book for little baby in evening at home, image ID: 102186786, belchonock.

Page 18   An overhead shot of an alert, 3 week old newborn baby boy looking at the camera, image ID: 22225004, katrinaelena.

Page 19   Young woman breastfeeding her little baby at home, image ID: 97726658, belchonock.

Page 25   Happy young mother and her baby in bed top view, image ID: 10980143, andreykuzmin.

Page 27   Close up portrait of a happy grandmother smiling with baby girl, image ID: 31624132, Michael Simons.

Page 33   Asian mother playing and taking care of baby at park, image ID: 74807624, Yupa Watchanakit.

Page 34   Small baby, looking to a mirror on bed, image ID: 2738254, Boris Ryaposov, 34.

Page 40   A woman with a baby play colourful toy in front of them, image ID: 42125456, Evgeniia Kuzmich.

Page 43   Family, fatherhood and people concept - red haired father and little baby daughter playing with soap bubbles at home, ID: 105477607, dolgachov.

Page 49   Happy young mother plays at hide-and-seek with her baby boy in a bed in a light bedroom of the house. Mother's Day. White , happy childhood, ID: 91320712, Guzel Andrianova.

Page 50   Cute baby girl plays with fruits with her father at home. The one-year child attentively looks at pear, ID: 64345837, Viacheslav Lopatin.

Page 51   Mom playing ball with baby indoor at home, image ID: 36834618, Oksana Kuzmina.

Page 57   Father washing a toddler in the bathroom at home, ID: 103091453, Jozef Polc.

Page 58   Young mother with her little daughter reading book, ID 15726088, petro.

Page 69   Little child playing with drawer, ID: 107534111, serezniy.

Page 70   Kid girl and mother playing together with cup toys, ID: 25067295, Oksana Kuzmina.

Page 71   Baby drawing with her hands, ID: 33700589, reana.

Page 80   Mom tickles the baby and has fun with him, ID: 103227436, oksix.

Page 86   Cute sock puppets isolated on white, ID: 14712466, serezniy.

Page 88   Happy mother holding baby boy at home, ID: 42592739, Wavebreak Media Ltd.

Page 98   Baby opening drawer with clothes on wooden furniture at home, ID: 65590017, Martin Novak.

Page 99   Child picking apples on a farm in autumn. Little baby boy playing in apple tree orchard. Kids pick fruit in a basket. Toddler eating fruits at fall harvest. Outdoor fun for children. Healthy nutrition, ID: 63589403, famveldman.

Page 100 Young hipster father playing with his daughter, ID: 39977323, Jozef Polc.

Page 101 Smiling baby girl eating food with mom on kitchen, ID: 36444763, Oksana Kuzmina.

Page 109 Portrait of funny cute white caucasian baby playing kinetic sand indoors at kindergarden. Early creativity brain development concept. Children home activity. Fine motor skills, ID: 81836153, Anna Kraynova.

Page 110 Young mom getting her baby girl dressed, ID: 18639845, Antonio Diaz.

Page 111 Baby girl waving hand, ID: 25178256, Leung Cho Pan.

Page 117 Beautiful young mother and daughter sitting on the floor next to a Christmas tree, playing and blowing balloons on a Christmas morning, ID: 90817074, Vladimir Cosic.

Page 118 Happy toddler boy playing with toys in his house, ID: 100908321, melpomen.

Page 119 Adorable boy with clothes of doctor is spoon-feeding teddy bear over white, ID: 12584067, Oksana Kuzmina.

ACKNOWLEDGEMENTS

There were many people that helped in the making of this book.

First, I would like to thank the parents I met both professionally and personally, who opened up and shared with me their unique child's journey from birth to first words. Your stories have helped make me a better speech-language pathologist and contributed greatly to shaping this book so that it may be useful to all kinds of families.

Secondly, I would like to thank the language researchers who tirelessly work to publish valuable clinical evidence so that people like myself, and other clinicians, can feel confident we are providing families with the best options and education available for their children.

Finally, a big thank you to my friend and editor, Jane Davies. You have helped turn my passion project into a true book and I will forever be grateful.

ABOUT THE AUTHOR

Lynn Carson is a speech-language pathologist and researcher. She received her master's degree in Communication Sciences and Disorders from Western University in Ontario, Canada, and has achieved clinical certification from Speech-Language and Audiology Canada. She is a member of the College of Audiologists and Speech-Language Pathologists of Ontario and Speech Pathology Australia. While this is her first book for parents, her clinical research has been published in peer reviewed journals in the United States and Canada. She is also the proud and busy mother of two children, currently completing her Ph.D. and residing in Sydney, Australia.

Made in the USA
Las Vegas, NV
10 September 2021